The Freedom Framework

"I would describe Cal as a 'People Expert' He intuitively knows how to help business owners build great culture while supporting a winning team spirit. In his book *The Freedom Framework* Cal shows you how to take your business to the next level. I believe inside each and every one of us is more than we can see—this book will help you unlock this in yourself, your business, and your people."

–**Joe Roberts**, The Push for Change

"Cal is passionate about helping others ensure they are doing the work they were meant to do. In *The Freedom Framework* Cal provides real-world, proven strategies on how to build the business of your dreams and live a more fulfilling life. I highly recommend that you lean on Cal's experience and read this book."

–**Brian Scrone**, Author of *What Matters Most* and co-founder of Family Board Meetings (familyboardmeetings.com)

"Over the course of his impressive career at TELUS, Cal was known for driving results and making significant contributions to our business. He is well known for his ability to build strong relationships across the organization, and I know the team benefited greatly from his passion and commitment to making TELUS a great place to work. When it comes to specific achievements in his role within the National Business Delivery team, there are many worth highlighting, the most significant being the focus and commitment he drove relating to our People & Culture strategy. In particular, Cal helped drive our engagement score from 54% in 2011 to 85% in 2015. I can assure you that the methodology found in *The Freedom Framework* is tried and true, and I have no doubt that reading this book can help you drive great results in your business also."

–**Marshall Berkin**, Vice President, Customer Relationship and Solutions Management, TELUS

"Cal Misener has a rare ability to see the big picture and provide the tools necessary to achieve that vision. I've worked with hundreds of entrepreneurs and business owners, but few have had the ability to cultivate culture, develop people, and optimize work flow like Cal does. If you run a business or are wanting to start one, this is a must-read!"

–**Connor Beaton**, Founder of Mantalks (www.mantalks.ca)

The
Freedom
Framework

THE BUSINESS OWNER'S
GUIDE TO EARNING MORE
AND WORKING LESS

CAL MISENER

NEW YORK

NASHVILLE • MELBOURNE • VANCOUVER

The Freedom Framework
THE BUSINESS OWNER'S GUIDE TO EARNING MORE AND WORKING LESS

Published in New York, New York, by Morgan James Publishing in partnership with Difference Press. Morgan James is a trademark of Morgan James, LLC. www.MorganJamesPublishing.com

The Morgan James Speakers Group can bring authors to your live event. For more information or to book an event visit The Morgan James Speakers Group at www.TheMorganJamesSpeakersGroup.com.

ISBN 978-1-68350-637-9 paperback
ISBN 978-1-68350-638-6 eBook
Library of Congress Control Number: 2017909697

Cover Design by:
Rachel Lopez
www.r2cdesign.com

Interior Design by:
Bonnie Bushman
The Whole Caboodle Graphic Design

In an effort to support local communities, raise awareness and funds, Morgan James Publishing donates a percentage of all book sales for the life of each book to Habitat for Humanity Peninsula and Greater Williamsburg.

Get involved today! Visit
www.MorganJamesBuilds.com

Dedication

I dedicate this book to all the business owners and leaders who have had the courage to start a business and follow their vision. It is my sincere hope that this book will help you make your own dreams for freedom and flexibility come true.

Table of Contents

Foreword

A chiropractor would believe that if your spine is not aligned the nervous system, as a result, cannot fire and perform correctly. I believe when you are not aligned in life you cannot feel fully alive to the possibilities that are in front of you and the ones that have yet to present themselves.

Misalignment is an epidemic in the world today. It appears to be getting worse with every passing year and is particularly prevalent in the workplace. We know what it feels like when we eat something that does not agree with the body. We know what it feels like when we wear shoes that are not the right fit. We know what it's like to date someone who is not aligned to who we are at the core.

Why is it, then, that our tolerance for misaligned work is unmatched?

Why do humans insist on staying for years in positions, roles, industries, and companies that are simply not aligned to their authentic selves?

Nature is a great and constant reminder of the importance of finding your element and hanging out there. Certain trees grow better in certain environments. Flowers blossom in places that nurture their individual beauty. One of the greatest examples of almost effortless and majestic beauty is the swan. One day, I heard the poet Davis Whyte speak about how majestic a swan is while it gracefully navigates the surface of the water in what appears to be a gliding motion. The swan has that upright pose that says, "Look at me. Notice how easy I make this look."

Take that swan out of water and it looks like a man who has just walked out of a pub after drinking way too much. It sways from side to side in what seems like an almost uncontrollable motion. On land, the swan seems to be saying, "Don't look at me."

Why do so many people admit to not being aligned to the work they do? Do they believe this is the way it has to be? Do they feel undeserving of work that nurtures their soul? Have they inherited a belief that work is more about making money in order to have more fun outside the office?

In my experience with coaching people, it's all of the above and more. What's scary is to total up the amount of awake time we spend working and look at the true cost of spending that time every day doing something that slowly erodes confidence and self-worth. The effect this has on relationships at home and, in many cases, also on physical health can be significant.

I believe that working without alignment has added to the overwhelming divorce rates sweeping the world right now. When we are not aligned in work, we often place greater expectations on the other elements in our lives to bring us even more meaning and fulfillment. The first thing I do with couples who are struggling is ask them how fulfilled they are in the other parts of their lives—where they live, the work they do, and regarding the most important relationship of all, the one with themselves.

In addition to the personal toll that working in a state of misalignment takes, there are costs to commercial productivity in the workplace that are almost so large as to be unquantifiable. Misalignment will affect workforce engagement. Just as engagement drives loyalty, misalignment will increase the turnover of people in a company.

There are so many books written each year that claim to show us how to grow a business, scale, and create culture. Getting to the next turnover level in business is such a focal point that what is often missing is the hidden cost of growth for growth's sake.

Cal's book is a holistic, real, and human approach to addressing these issues around the disconnection and misalignment many people experience in the workplace, starting at the top with company leadership. What makes

Cal the perfect messenger and advocate of alignment in the workplace is that he has openly and courageously admitted that he has spent most of his working life in a corporate position that did not connect with who he really is. His realization that, in part, the misalignment at work was driven by a deep disconnection within himself showcases why he is the messenger we need to listen to, because he has gone on to solve this issue for himself, help others solve it for themselves, and now has given us a book on the topic.

I was fortunate to get to witness part of Cal's transformation through the lens of my documentary film *Give & Grow* (to find out more about Cal's journey and the documentary, go to www.giveandgrowfilm.com). We followed Cal on a journey of self-discovery, clarifying the truth about his own misalignment, and the courageous pivot he made on his journey. It's his own personal journey and transition that make Cal's message that much more authentic and real.

Philip McKernan
Speaker, Author, and Filmmaker

INTRODUCTION

Achieving Success in All Areas of Your Business

The success of a business can be measured in multiple currencies. Money or cash flow is the obvious one, but many business owners also want their business to provide freedom in terms of time and not being geographically constrained. Imagine a world where you were vastly exceeding all of the financial targets *and* you were free to travel, do the things you love, and have your business support that lifestyle.

Another measure of success, one that is not talked about as much, is alignment that leads to fulfillment. In simple terms, alignment is doing work that you love. This is arguably the most important measurement of success. If you have a business that is earning money and affording you some freedom and flexibility but you hate it, what is the point? As solopreneurs or small business owners, we often end up having to do everything in our businesses ourselves, at least when we're starting out. There are typically aspects of our business that we really enjoy and parts that we do not. How do we set things up so that we focus more on the things we enjoy and have a real sense of meaningful alignment? We will dive into this further later in the book.

Here is a list of the success measures mentioned above:

- **Fulfillment**—Being aligned with the work we do, and doing what energizes us
- **Financial**—Obviously, we want to make money in our business
- **Freedom**—Having time to do the things we love to do, while knowing that our business is being taken care of
- **Flexibility**—Being able to work and live where we want to and not be "chained" to any one location.

The good news is that a business can be set up to make money, free up time, and also provide the flexibility to travel. However, this can rarely be accomplished without a winning team. As a business owner, you can also have a real sense of fulfillment by getting to do the work that energizes you the most within your business and getting help with the parts that do not. Having a group of people (even if it's a group of one to start with!) supporting your business and being emotionally invested in your success is what leads to not feeling like your business is a "ball and chain."

Creating a winning team to support your business goals may seem obvious for a larger company, but this can also apply to smaller companies and even to solopreneurs.

How Can Having A Team Actually Help?

Let me give you an example of how having a good team of people can help. Let's say you're a real estate professional and don't currently have anyone supporting you. Adding one or two key people to assist you can make a huge difference. Imagine that 50% of your time was spent on admin and support functions and the other 50% of your time was spent on finding and closing deals. For this example, let's say you were doing one deal per month, for a total of twelve deals for the year. If you were able to get some help with the administrative tasks so that you could focus exclusively on generating revenue, you could potentially do 24 deals a year and double your income, even while working less on the things that do not bring as much value to your business.

Here's a graphic to show that alignment (doing what you love and having others support the areas within your business that you don't love quite as much) can lead to financial gain, time freedom, and flexibility around how and where you work.

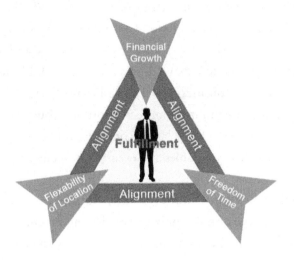

Throughout this book, we will look at the importance of aligning to the work you are passionate about and/or that generates the most value to your business, and then getting help with the stuff that doesn't necessarily light you up.

This book will help you set up your business to give you more financial and time freedom, as well as the flexibility to work where you want to. The book is divided into two parts. Part 1 focuses on alignment. We'll go through the process of identifying your "theme" or the things in your business that you need to be focused on. Part 1 includes a way to help you ensure the people who work for you are also aligned. Part 2 focuses on supporting a team of people. Once you have found the right people—people who are passionate about what they do and will support your business—you can use a "roadmap" to ensure your people continue to get the support they need.

By using the tools in Part 1 and Part 2 you can build your own freedom framework.

The Deeper Journey

Before going to Part 1, I would like to tell you more about how I got here and why I am so passionate about meaningful alignment. I'll do that in the next chapter.

What the next chapter doesn't tell you about specifically is the deeper and more personal journey that was required for me to step into a job role that was much more suited to me. I bring this up because your own process of pursuing alignment in your business, for both yourself and your team, may require you to grow and become aware on deeper personal levels, too.

In this book, the main focus is on finding alignment in your work and supporting your team in their alignment. This is important because we spend a significant portion of our lives doing work. However, some deeper personal work may be required in order to truly realize alignment in all areas of your life.

CHAPTER 1

A People and Culture Champion Is Born

In this first chapter, I want to give you a bit of background about myself and how I ended up working with other business owners and leaders to help them deliver extraordinary results by ensuring they are focused on the aspects of their business that they love and are getting help with the things they don't.

What Is My Thing?

Having a sense of fulfillment in your business starts with knowing about the things you are passionate about. Here's the story of how I found "my thing."

When I was getting out of high school, I had absolutely no idea what I wanted to do career-wise (even life-wise for that matter!). The closest I came to even having an inkling as to what that would be was wanting to become a commercial airline pilot. Travel was, and is, one of my passions, so I thought perhaps I could be a pilot and travel the world. Unfortunately, I also had a perception at the time that there was no way I could afford to get a commercial license. When I see now what many people pay for a post-secondary education of any kind, I realize that the cost of becoming a pilot was not outlandish. At the time, it seemed too far out of reach for me.

I don't recall anyone asking me what I was really passionate about. I was not aware of any process I could go through to try and determine that. Like a lot of young people, I simply tried a bunch of stuff to see if any of them were "my thing." I worked in a warehouse. I worked as a laborer cleaning up rig sites. I worked moving mobile homes. I was a dishwasher, pipeline leak consultant, fuel transfer technician (gas jockey), etc., etc., etc. The longest stint I had in any one role was as a pipeline consultant, traveling to different parts of Canada. I thought, at the time, that if I could make some money and do a bit of traveling, I would be fulfilled. I soon realized that money didn't lead to satisfaction, and traveling to many rural small towns in Western Canada and the Northwest Territories was not exactly the travel I had envisioned!

I eventually was hired by the Canadian telecommunications company TELUS and held a variety of technical and operational roles as a technician and then as a people leader, leading operational teams. To keep a long story somewhat shorter, I will not go into all of the roles I had. Let's say they were all technical in nature, and I realized that was not my thing. I was with TELUS for a total of 21 years, and approximately fifteen of those years were in technical/operational roles.

Since I knew that technical work in telecommunications was not what I was passionate about, I started a variety of small businesses while working at TELUS, including a grocery home delivery service, an Internet marketing company, and a real estate investment company. I was looking for freedom, flexibility, and—most of all—fulfillment. I wanted to feel a sense of alignment and to feel good about the work I was doing.

I soon realized there were aspects of each of these sideline endeavors that I enjoyed, but there were parts that I did not enjoy. In my real estate business, for example, I was able to build up a multimillion-dollar portfolio, but I had to spend a lot of time on admin, bookkeeping, maintenance, dealing with tenants, and other things that I didn't really like doing. Most of those tasks were not what I'd had in mind for my "dream business." I was financially successful, but didn't feel much in the way of freedom, because I had to deal with all aspects of my business—not only the aspects I enjoyed—and that left me feeling like I simply had found myself another job. I also did not feel a sense of fulfillment, as I realized that while there were definitely parts of the business that I loved, such as meeting new people and finding the next deal, working on all the other administrative tasks associated with an investment business was definitely not my thing.

At one stage when I was at TELUS, I was leading a team of technical people doing very technical work. While I absolutely loved leadership and supporting that team of people, I was not passionate about the technology side of things.

At this point in my career, I felt a little disoriented and I didn't know why. I'd done everything I was supposed to do. I'd gone to school, gotten good marks, was hired by a great company, received full benefits and a pension plan, started my own businesses in the process, and had achieved the title and pay that I had hoped for. I had invested my money in real estate and the stock market and done all the things that I had been told would make me successful. Why did it not feel right?

I now realize that the feeling I was experiencing was misalignment in my life. I was not doing work that I was meant to do. I learned that the fulfillment I was seeking definitely did not come in the form of title, pay, benefits, or any of those things. I didn't even really know exactly what I was meant to do; however, I did know that the hollow feeling I was experiencing was not going to work for me. I knew that doing work that did not feed my soul was not something I was willing to tolerate any longer. In the absence of knowing exactly what I was going to do, I took some steps in a new direction.

This is the story of the first step I took in order to feel more aligned with the work I was doing.

My boss was a gentleman named Dave, who was the Vice President of our area, and I remember having an epiphany one day. I just knew in my gut that I needed to do something that was more fulfilling, so I called Dave and we had a conversation that went something like this:

Me: "Hi, Dave, it's Cal."

Dave: "Hi, Cal."

Me: "Hey, you know all that technical stuff I've been doing? Well, I don't want to do that anymore."

Dave (being a good leader, a friend, and one of my best mentors): "Okay. What is it that you *do* want to do?"

Me: "I want to support your team, but from a people and culture point of view."

Dave: "Okay then, you got it."

I really didn't even know what it meant to support a team of people "from a people and culture point of view." All I knew was that the technical work was not doing it for me and my passion seemed to lie with helping others achieve what they wanted to achieve in their own careers. I was starting to get glimpses of real *fulfillment* in my role by supporting other people's growth and helping them with alignment.

Can I Do This By Myself?

Trying to be everything to everyone within a role or a business can be tiring and does not make sense. There were certain activities that I loved to do, and they seemed effortless; and others felt like absolute drudgery. What I was learning was that by building the right team, I could work more on the things that excited me and less on the things that didn't.

I'd had a lot of great mentors throughout my career (Dave being one of the most significant), and I felt like I was in a position to help others just as I had been helped. Although I was not excited about doing technical work myself, I was *very* excited about helping others get into the careers they wanted to be in, doing work they were excited about, getting the training and development they needed, and basically ensuring that our team was engaged and passionate about what they were doing. Dave was a visionary leader who realized that the way to deliver on the business results he was looking for was through supporting a great team—and that I could help him achieve that goal.

Dave had a team of approximately 700 people across the country at that time, and he was willing to create a role for me, at my suggestion, that was specifically to help build a great culture by supporting a great team. In a company of approximately 42,000 people, it is very rare, if not unheard of, for someone to create a role for themselves in the way that I had.

I was not only an employee at TELUS and an entrepreneur with my own businesses. I was also an "intrapreneur." Even though my official title at TELUS was Manager of Planning and Engineering, I considered my new title to be People and Culture Champion. I was responsible for helping create and drive our cultural roadmap, which is fancy way of saying that my job was to try to ensure that our team was a cool group to be in, and that people on our team got to do work they were excited about.

One of the first things Dave and I discussed was implementing the idea of meaningful alignment so that people would be able align their personal passions with the work they were doing, which would, in turn, help us deliver on the business objectives that our team was working toward. In that new role, I was demonstrating to others that if I could create a role for myself that I liked better, then they could do the same. By identifying what I was passionate about and then working to align that with the business' needs, I discovered that a person really *could* have fulfillment—and it didn't come from pay, or a fancy title, or any of those types of things. The fulfillment came from doing work I was actually meant to do. I created a framework to help others on the team do the same and rolled it out to 70 managers and over 700 team members. I coached leaders on how to have conversations around alignment, did some discovery around people's passions in a team environment, and then we determined how to align those findings with the work that the team was responsible for.

That new role of supporting the team involved a number of different aspects. Here is a list of some of the functions I was responsible for:

- Team leadership
- Data analysis
- Communication
- Learning and development
- Content creation
- Administration

The challenge with delivering on all of these functions was that I was only one person. I did not have the bandwidth, nor the desire, to do all of those different things myself, so I knew I needed to get help. I was passionate about team leadership and sharing the vision of where we were going as an organization, but I was not passionate about many of the other tasks that my new role involved. I knew that the way to accomplish all of those things and be successful was to surround myself with people who were passionate about doing the things I was not.

How do you build a team? One person at a time. I started by having a support person who could help me with administrative tasks, like scheduling and reporting, so I could focus on the development of the vision and the plan for the team. Once that initial support person was on board, I had the freedom and flexibility to focus on the things I was passionate about. Together, we did a much better job of delivering on our overall results than I would have done on my own.

Eventually, my own team at TELUS grew, and I was able to hire more people to support some of the other areas of the business that I was responsible for. I looked at everything that

I was responsible for delivering, looked at the things I was good at that brought me energy, and then looked at how I could get help with the things I was not as passionate about. The key was to hire people who were good at and excited about the parts of the business that I was not. By hiring the right people, I was able to deliver on the things we were responsible for overall, but spend the majority of my time doing work that I actually enjoyed.

Initially, I had a limited budget for hiring full-time people, so I looked for creative ways to get help. I did hire some full-time team members, but I also got people to do some work while on loan to my area, so that I did not have to hire full-time people but was still able to get the help I needed. When it did not make sense to hire a full-time person, I hired people on a contract basis to help out with particular projects. I engaged summer students who could help out, as well, at a minimum cost. I even had some resources in the Philippines and India who contributed to the overall goals for our team. The cool thing was that I was able to manage that team remotely, since we were all in different geographic locations.

Can I Work From Anywhere?

With technology what it is today, it is not as important as it used to be to always work from one location. There are reliable and inexpensive tools available that can bridge the location gap. Sure, there are times when we physically need to be in a certain place, but by having the right systems and—

most importantly—the right people in place, we gain much more geographical flexibility.

In my new role at TELUS I had an office in downtown Vancouver, which I initially went to five days a week, because I thought I needed to be there in order to support my team. TELUS had implemented something called Work Styles that allowed team members to work from home, at least a portion of the time. I realized, over time, that even though I was going in to the office five days a week, my team was starting to work more and more from home, so maybe I didn't need to be physically present in the office as much as I previously had. Within my team, we implemented something we called Work at Work Wednesdays, so that everybody who worked locally would be in the office at one point during the week. It can be important to be physically together, with some degree of frequency, in order to stay in touch with each other as a team. At one point, in addition to the local team members, we had team members in Victoria, Vernon, Vancouver, Calgary, Toronto, and Montreal, as well as overseas, and we were all able to work together to contribute to the team's success.

The team members—including me—were doing work that we enjoyed, and we were able to work from home more and more often, which gave us all more flexibility. I wanted to experiment to see if I could work away from the office for an extended period of time, so that I didn't necessarily have to be in Vancouver. My only real criteria for working remotely was reliable Internet access, so that I could be online and support the team as required, and have access to conference calling, voicemail, etc.

In 2011, I did a first trial of working from a geographic location besides my home office or my office in downtown Vancouver. I went to Mexico for three weeks as a test. For the most part, that trial was a success. However, the challenge I had (and the thing I needed the most!) was having a reliable Internet connection. The place I stayed had advertised dedicated Internet access in the suite itself. That sounded perfect to me, because it meant I could stay at my desk in the condo and conduct my work day just as I would from home or my office in Vancouver. The challenge was that the Internet in my suite worked only part of the time. The rest of the time, it was completely down. I found that the shared access in the lobby worked much more reliably.

One day, when I was still in Mexico, I was scheduled to lead a call of 70 people, and I thought it would be no problem. I would use my phone application on my laptop, dial in from the shared access in the lobby, and lead the call. I dialed into the conference bridge and gradually people started to join the call. Everything was great. I kicked off the meeting, the sound quality was good, I could hear all of the participants, and they could hear me. I was even able to share my screen with people located from coast to coast in Canada. I was proud of myself and the trial so far... until the mariachi band started playing in the lobby!

The band came strolling in and were playing at a considerable volume, which kind of ruined my plan to work from the lobby. Fortunately, I was able to get someone from my team to take over the call and finish it up, because I could not even hear myself think over the band. This story speaks to some of the challenges with working remotely, but also to the power of having a strong team that you can rely on, since they were able to finish the call on my behalf.

In subsequent years, I found better solutions for reliable Internet access, and for the last five years in a row I have spent two months each winter working from Hawaii, for TELUS and on my own business. The only way I could accomplish that was by having the right people on the team supporting me, so that, together, we could ensure everything was being taken care of.

I really felt like I had achieved my success measures of *flexibility* and *freedom*. Most importantly, I had a sense of fulfillment from doing work I enjoyed. Financially I was doing well and was meeting the goals I had set out for myself.

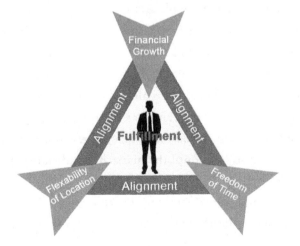

By surrounding myself with people who were good at the things that I wasn't so good at, I was starting to gain more freedom with my time to do more of the things I wanted to do. I also had a lot more flexibility in general, as I wasn't trying to do everything myself.

Summary

As business owners, we can have financial success, but we can also have flexibility and freedom. It starts by knowing the areas of your business you want to be focused on, and then figuring out how to get help with the remainder. This also leads to satisfaction and fulfillment, because you get to spend your time on the things you enjoy the most.

Building a great team of people who support your vision and business is the key to success. Whatever the size of your organization or your team, the same principles apply. Perhaps your business currently consists of only yourself or a very small number of people who work directly or indirectly for you. Even so, success depends on you doing what you love and are good at, and having others help you with all the other aspects.

Reflection

- What percentage of your time is spent doing work you love versus doing work you feel you have to do?
- How can you get help in your business with the work you are not passionate about, in order to give yourself more flexibility and freedom?

PART 1

ALIGNMENT

As mentioned in the Introduction, this book is divided into two main parts. This first part focuses on alignment, on doing work you are passionate about and ensuring that those who work for you are passionate about what they do also.

Part 2 will give you the framework to support a winning team in helping you deliver in all areas of your business.

CHAPTER 2

Delivering on Your Success Measures

We can measure success in business in a number of ways, including financial gain, feeling fulfilled by the work we do, having time to focus on the things that are important to us, as well as having the flexibility to be mobile and live/work in different locations. This can all be accomplished by having a plan that sets you up for success.

What Does Good Look Like?

In order to ensure that your business is set up to deliver on all of those measures of success, it's important to have a framework that you can follow. Being fulfilled in the work you do begins with being conscious about the things you are passionate about and the things you are not passionate about within your business. Once you know the things you enjoy doing versus the things you don't, you know the areas you need help with. Even if your team is small or consists of one other person, to start with, you can focus on alignment for yourself and supporting those you hire to help you to be in alignment, too. When you have some key people in place, your framework or "people plan" will help you to ensure that they remain happy and passionate about what they are doing.

Working in my new role at TELUS, I felt more aligned than I had at any other time in my career, because I was doing work I was very passionate about. I was supporting Dave and his team with all things "people and culture." We knew that to be successful as a team and meet our business objectives we needed to get our people in the right roles doing work that they enjoyed and that, overall, they needed to feel like the company and our team was a cool place to work.

The first step that journey was alignment. On the next page is a model that illustrates this idea of alignment.

The whole idea behind this concept of "meaningful alignment" is to, first, make sure we're doing work we enjoy, and then to help people who work for us do work they enjoy, but also help them understand the contribution they can make to the larger team, and thus contribute to your overall business objectives.

In the model, there are three main areas of influence, each represented by a circle. The first area is "Me"—who you are as an individual, what is important to you, what kinds

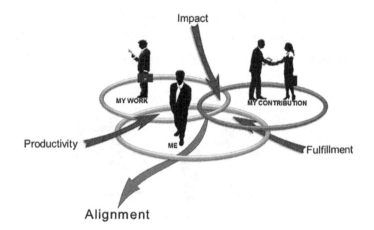

Alignment

of things you are passionate about, your skills and strengths, and what you bring to the table. The second circle is "My Work"—your role, what types of things you are doing, and—most importantly—what you're excited about that you get to do on a daily basis. For example, if meeting new people and discussing new deals or new opportunities is "your thing," how do you set up the running of your business so that you can do more of that and less of what doesn't excite you?

The intersection between those two circles is labeled "Production," which is the result or expected output as those two areas interact. "Production" simply means that whatever work you are responsible for, there is a certain output. If you are in sales, for example, the "Production" may be the number of sales calls you perform in a day. This intersection would be considered "table stakes"—a basic function that you get paid for as part of your job. There are many levels to job satisfaction, and this "Production," or output, is the most basic level of job satisfaction that comes from putting out what you being paid to do (e.g., making those sales calls each day).

In the model, the intersection between "My Work" and "My Contribution" leads to "Impact."

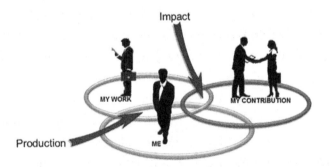

When you are doing work that you enjoy but you also understand your contribution and how you're helping meet overall business objectives, you have a sense of the impact you can have on the business.

A third intersection is between "Me" and "My Contribution," and the outcome at this intersection is "Fulfillment."

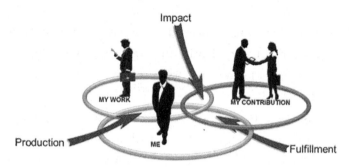

When you know the contribution you're making and it's in line with what's important to you personally, you get a profound sense of fulfillment.

Finally, when all three of these areas are well developed, it creates a true sense of "Meaningful Alignment."

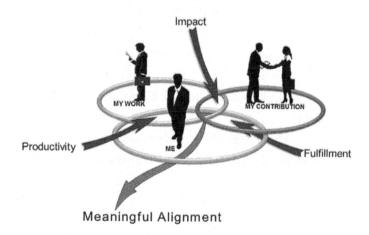

In having this sense of alignment, you know what is important to you personally and what lights you up. You can then ensure you are doing work that aligns with your personal "theme," as well as with your talents and strengths. You know how the work you enjoy contributes to your business and you can identify the areas you want help with and what types of people to hire so they are passionate about what they do also.

This whole idea of alignment is critical to accomplishing your goals and feeling fulfillment within your business. You can probably think of a time in your own career when you were doing work that you were not excited about. When I think back to doing the technical work at TELUS, I know that it was not something I was personally passionate about, so it was difficult for me to motivate my team and to stay motivated myself. It was also difficult for me to understand the impact I was having, and I certainly did not feel a profound sense of fulfillment, since the work I was doing on a daily basis was not my thing. When I started to focus on the people side of things, however, doing what I loved to do, it became much easier for me to understand the impact I could have and, as a result, I definitely felt more aligned and fulfilled.

Once you have aligned things for *yourself* in your business, it is important to help facilitate that for the people who are either working for you already or who you want to hire. If you have people doing work that lights them up, they will generate amazing results for you.

Alignment is the critical first step in supporting a team and building a great business. Are you as a leader doing what you enjoy doing and are you helping others also find work they love? Are you helping them understand the impact they can make and checking in to make sure they are fulfilled and feeling like they're doing what they were meant to do? If everyone in your organization is passionate about the work they do, this will definitely impact your customers.

Once we have this sense of alignment for ourselves and for others, then what?

How Do I Support a Winning Team?

Later in the book, in Part 2, we'll go into detail about how to support your team. For now, we'll look at an overview of what you can do to support them.

Over and above meaningful alignment, there are five other key areas of focus to ensure that you have happy, passionate, engaged team members supporting your business. Whether you are an experienced leader or people leadership is not your thing, you can follow this framework to help the people supporting you get what they need. The five areas of the framework are shown in the figure on the previous page.

We will review each section of this "people plan" model in great detail in the coming chapters.

By ensuring alignment for yourself and your team and then having an overarching plan in place to support your people, you can accomplish anything in your business. 90% of leaders think that having a strategy to support their team has an impact on their business, yet only 25% of them actually have one (Officevibe, 2014). Having a plan to support your team will help you achieve the things you want to achieve with your business. This is a total win-win situation.

There are a few key reasons that having an overall people plan is important. The first reason is that having a detailed plan will keep you on track as a leader who wants to be the best they can be at supporting their team. In order to have fulfillment in the work you do, it is important to be able to focus on the things that energize you, and get help with the stuff that does not. Having a plan to support your team— whether the team consists of one person or 100 people—will give you more time to focus on the things that are important to you and that bring value to your business. Finally, having key people in place who are supported and who are passionate about what they do can allow you to live and work for extended periods of time away from your where your business is geographically located.

A sound people plan includes the five elements shown on the model above. People need to enjoy their work and understand their contribution. They need to feel recognized and also receive consistent communication so they know what is going on with the company and they know where they stand. They need to understand the career potential they have and what possibilities may be in store for them in the future. They need to have opportunities for growth and to have a sense that their ongoing development will improve your business in the process. Finally, there needs to be an element of contribution and giving back. One of most basic means of feeling fulfillment as a human being is to help other human beings.

If you are offering all of these things to your team on a consistent basis, that is how you build a rockstar team of people who support your business as if it was their own.

Summary

You can have your cake and eat it too. By ensuring that you are aligned to work that you enjoy and that you have help in your business for all other areas, you can get a real sense of fulfillment from the work you do. When you are supported in your business by other passionate people, you can deliver on all of your other success measures, including financial growth, freedom, and flexibility.

Reflection

- What can you do to focus more on the things that excite you and focus less on the things that don't?
- What areas of your business should you be delegating or getting some help with?

CHAPTER 3

Meaningful Alignment Starts With You

In this chapter, we will review this concept of alignment and how doing work that lights you up leads to a more fulfilling life and helps you improve all areas of your business.

Why Meaningful Alignment?

The secret to happiness in business and in life is alignment. Are you doing work that you were meant to do? Do you get out of bed energized in the morning? Or do you drag your feet and say, *Not another day in the office*? We spend approximately two-thirds of our adult lives working, so it is critical that we enjoy at least most aspects of what we do. It is also extremely difficult to support someone who works for you with their own alignment if you haven't experienced alignment for yourself.

When I was working at TELUS and I started to shift away from doing technical work that I was not all that excited about and leaning more towards my passion of supporting other people's growth and transformation, something very interesting started to happen. I found the small team of people that I supported were very inspired by the fact that I could make a shift toward doing what I loved. My title had not officially changed, but I had started to focus more on what I really wanted to do and to delegate the parts of my role that I didn't enjoy. At that point, I basically had two distinct roles within the company: I supported a small team of fourteen technical people, and I was developing my role as the People and Culture Champion to support the broader team of 700 people.

One example of how I was able to shift away from one thing in order to focus on another and become more aligned was how I helped one of the individuals on my smaller team become the acting manager of that team so that I could focus on my newly created people role. That person had expressed an interest in getting into a leadership role, so it was a win-win situation. I helped him move toward what *he* wanted to do which, in turn, helped me move more toward what *I* wanted to do.

In leading by example and focusing more on the things that I was passionate about, I started to get the team thinking about what shifts they could make, and how we could all feel more aligned with the work we did.

Attracting top talent to support your business would be virtually impossible to do if you as the leader were not passionate about the work you do. The real power of having a team is that you can identify all of the things that you need to accomplish together, identify who is good at what (and also passionate about those things), and ensure that you align the work you need to accomplish with the strengths of your team. According to Officevibe, a company that helps other business owners measure their employee satisfaction, 80% of senior managers are not passionate about the work they do (Shriar, 2016). If a leader is not passionate about the work they do, how can they facilitate that for others?

Whether you have a large team or you have yet to hire your first person, your sense alignment is what brings you fulfillment but it is also what will lead to people sticking around. I have had people come to work for me who took a significant cut in pay simply because they wanted to be part of a winning team and because they got to focus on work that excited them.

How Do I Know What Lights Me Up?

I always envied people who knew at a very young age what they wanted to do for work or business. Even if we know the type of business we want to start or the type of career we want to have, how often do we stop to think about how we want to spend our time each day? For example, if you wanted to become a realtor, did you consider all of the tasks involved in closing a real estate deal? There are the obvious tasks, such as meeting with clients and negotiating deals, but a number of other tasks are also involved, such as making sure the paperwork is completed properly and managing your schedule and calendar to keep track of the different meetings you have. Once a deal has been signed, it can move into a repeatable process flow so that it can be scaled and repeated. Do you have help with this already? Or do you need to perform all of those steps yourself?

Action Steps

I have found that people don't always know exactly what things excite them about the work they do. This is not necessarily because of apathy, but could be because of not having taken the time to reflect on such things. The Freedom Framework helps business owners and leaders figure this piece out for themselves, and also helps them figure this out for the people they support. In the Alignment Workshop that we deliver, we ask a number of simple but powerful questions to help people identify what is important to them and then help them shift toward doing more of that kind of work.

Doing the exercises below will help you to determine how you would like to best spend your time during a work day.

These exercises can be quite powerful. They are simple, but their power comes from taking the time to reflect on what is really important to us. Try answering the questions for yourself, and giving them to the people who work for you, so they can benefit from them, too.

Exercise

What does a perfect day at work look like for you? "Perfect" is a strong word, but think of an awesome day you had at work. What made it so great? What things did you focus the majority of your time on during that day? Who were you with?

When you reflect on your answers, note how often you have a "perfect" day at work or, at least, how often you spend time doing the things that excite you.

Exercise

What lights you up? What kinds of things give you energy as opposed to take it away? What is a topic that, once you start talking about it, you can't stop or you get really excited and animated?

Having A Theme

We will dive more into this idea of having a theme in the next chapter. I believe everybody has a "theme" for the things that bring them satisfaction at work. For example, my theme is around connection—networking with new people; getting reacquainted with people I haven't seen for a while; inspiring my team to do their best; working with others to create new and exciting possibilities. Those are the activities that excite me. No matter what role I'm in, which client I'm working with, or whether I'm in a business or personal situation, the days that I live my theme of connection, are the most meaningful to me.

I recall coming home from work one day and I was almost bouncing off the walls I was so excited. My wife said, "You look like you had an incredible day at work today. What happened?" At TELUS, we had moved to doing a Work Styles program, whereby it was possible for team members to work from home for a portion of time and work in the office a portion of the time. We had certain office spaces that were reconfigured into a hotel business station type of arrangement, whereby a desk could be reserved in a particular area and shared with others who had also made reservations. The neat thing about that arrangement was that on any given day in the office there would be new people and people from all areas of the company.

On the day I came home and my wife noticed how energized I was, there had not been anything earth-shattering that had happened. What was happening, though, was I was living my theme of connection, in that I had met a bunch of new people that I had not previously known and I had found out about some cool projects they were working on. I'd also met one person who worked in a different city, whom I had spoken with over the phone many times over the years but had never met in person.

This idea of connecting with people is what excites me and I know I need to do more of in the work place in order to feel engaged.

After running hundreds of people through a workshop about alignment, these are some of the more common themes that come up for people:

- Creativity
- Connection
- Problem-solving
- Teaching
- Technology
- Negotiating

Do you know what your theme is? Do you know what your team members' themes are? If not, do not fear, as we will uncover that in the next chapter!

What about the Stuff That Doesn't Light Me Up?

In addition to discovering your theme and how you want to spend a good portion of your workday, one of the most powerful tools for fulfillment for us as leaders is *delegation*. Delegating helps us focus on the things we enjoy and are good at and get help with the things that we may not enjoy.

As a business owner, particularly a small business owner, we typically have held every role within the company, at least initially. A real sense of freedom can come from focusing on the work that gives you energy as opposed to takes it away, and then getting help from others to do the work that you are not passionate about.

I know that my theme is connection, so that is where I should spend the majority of my time, but I also know that there is a long list of things that I should not be focused on, because they do not help me stay in alignment. Delegation can be a great way to accomplish alignment for leaders.

Summary

It is key as a leader to feel a sense of alignment in the work you do. Being focused on the things that excite you and getting help with the things that do not will lead to greater work satisfaction. There may be things you have to do that you don't enjoy as much as other things, but you can ask yourself if you are spending the majority of your time on things you enjoy, and are thus leveraging your skills. In order to have a highly engaged, inspired, and aligned team, you need to first feel that way yourself. Then you can translate that to help the people you support, also become aligned.

Reflection

- What lights you up in your business? If you don't know, what can you do to determine that?
- What percentage of your daily work activities do you actually enjoy? What are the activities you would rather not do?

CHAPTER 4

Passion Is Key

In order to deliver great results in all areas of your business, it is important that the people who support you are passionate about what they do. You can hire based a number of different criteria, but having people who are passionate about the things you are not as passionate about in your business is key.

In this chapter, we will discuss how to ensure that the people on your team like what they do. We will also discuss a framework for how to continually check in with them.

How Do I Help Others with Their Own Alignment?

Having employees who are passionate about what they do can be very powerful. Here is an example of the positive results that can come when you help unlock that passion for someone.

In addition to supporting the broader team of 700 people in my new role as the People and Culture Champion at TELUS, I still had a small team of technical people who reported directly to me. I felt like I was able to completely transform my role within a large organization and I got curious about whether or not I could facilitate something similar for the people who reported directly to me. I wanted to ensure that they were doing work they were excited about and, if not, I wanted to see what I could do to help them have the same sense of alignment that I had achieved for myself.

I typically met with each of my team members every month. We would discuss their performance as well as have a conversation about their careers and what they wanted in the longer term. (If you don't currently have at least a monthly or bi-monthly scheduled discussion with each person you support, I highly recommend it as a best practice within an overall people plan. More to come on this later!)

I started asking the team members I met with different questions than the ones I had asked in the past. I asked them, "What really lights you up?" and "Why do you come to work each day?" and "If you had your dream job, what would that be?" Those were not standard performance management questions. People started to look forward to our monthly discussions, because we talked genuinely about them and what they wanted to do with their lives and careers; and how I could help them get to where they wanted to go.

Those regular discussions were going well, and I thought everything was on track, but then I got a surprise call from Michael.

Michael was one of my top performers and I would have been lost without him. I thought I was being a very supportive leader by asking people what they specifically wanted to do. What I had yet to discover was that it's sometimes very difficult for someone to give specifics about what they want to *do*, because their job fulfillment is more attached to their theme or what I call their way of being. This way of being is about how they want to behave every day or what *types* of things—not necessarily specifics—bring them fulfillment. For Michael, that theme was creativity. He was extremely creative and artistic, and if he wasn't living within that theme, he felt like he was dying inside.

Once we've figured out what our theme is (if we didn't already know), we can really start to structure the work we do to fit within that theme, which ultimately brings us much more gratification than pay rate, title, or some of those other motivators. (We will get into this more later on in the book.)

Here is a portion of a call I had with Michael:

Michael: "Cal, it's Michael. I think I need to leave TELUS."

Me   (with complete shock and dismay in my
          voice): "What do you mean you need to leave
          TELUS?"

Michael: "The work you have me doing isn't cutting it
          for me, so I think I need to go elsewhere."
          (That illustrates how misalignment can lead to
          losing top talent, which is not good. We will
          also cover more on this topic later on in the
          book.)

Me: "What if you don't need to leave TELUS?
          What if you don't even need to leave this team
          or have a different job title? What if we just
          get you doing work that you're more excited
          about?"

Michael: "I can't imagine what that would look like, Cal. I
          trust you, so I will have that conversation with
          you, but I'm not sure what I could possibly do
          for work here that's going to satisfy me."

Michael and I did have that conversation. We followed
what has by now become a well-defined framework in order
to discover his theme of creativity. Once we had established
that, we were able to work together to match the needs of the
business with his passion around being creative.

One of the things I wanted to do to support the broader
team of 700 people was to celebrate our successes as a team.
But I didn't want to do it in a typical corporate, stuffy,
"talking head" fashion. I wanted something impactful

and emotional that would strike a chord with our team members. Michael and I talked about him creating a mid-year video that would accomplish that, as a way for us fulfill the need for a celebration video and to leverage his creative talents.

Michael went away and worked on a draft of the video. He utilized all of his creative talents and came up with what he thought was going to meet the mark. He sent me a link to the draft and it was truly amazing! I watched the video and I actually started to cry, because it was so impactful. It was exactly what I had hoped it would be! I phoned Michael and when he answered the phone, my exact words were, "Are you frigging kidding me?" Understandably, he said, "What? Did I do something wrong?" I said, "No, you did nothing wrong. The video is absolutely amazing! I am almost speechless it's so good."

We went on to release the finished video to our broader team, and it was met with a wonderfully positive reception. Other teams within TELUS heard about the video and started asking how we'd done it. They started reaching out to Michael to find out more.

The truly inspiring thing about that story is not even the video. It is fast-forwarding to Michael's situation eighteen months after that video. Michael went from wanting to leave our company to feeling like he had won the lottery, because he was doing the creative work he yearned to do. Our business was better off because we had put Michael's creative talents to work.

There is a bit of a funny footnote to that story. About six months after we released that first video, Michael was working on other creative endeavors that support the business, such as creating a dashboard for my team to show our results, but in a very cool, creative way. Michael would email or ping me—even on a Saturday evening at 11 p.m.—because he was so excited about a new tool or piece of software he had discovered. I would have to tell him to curb his enthusiasm over the weekend, but that I would love to hear more about it on Monday morning.

Tapping into that kind of passion—having someone on board who is so excited about their work that they use their discretionary time to do more of it—can be invaluable to your business. Michael had always been a great employee, but when he was doing work that he was excited about, his productivity went through the roof.

Just as I have a theme around connection and Michael has a theme around creativity, we all have a theme.

Action Steps

Below is another exercise from our Alignment workshop that is very powerful. It's about defining one's passion. I encourage you to go through this exercise for yourself, but it's also a great exercise to do with your team members to see what makes them tick.

The first time I did this exercise with my team, the experience was *hugely* powerful. I learned things about the people I supported, and they learned a lot about each other also. For example, I worked with one man on my team for years. For the entire time I had known him, he had been doing very technical work and I always saw him as a tech guy. As part of this passion exercise, I discovered that one of his passions was art and that in his spare time, he was an online art critic! Who knew? When we find out about each others' passions as a team, we built deeper connections with each other. As a leader, I got some great insight into how I could support people at much deeper levels. Having that insight into what people were passionate about also allowed me to ensure they were focused on the right work. That, in turn, would help me deliver maximum results for the business.

This exercise can be very impactful for a small business owner. You can first identify what activities you should be focused on based on your passions but can also use this when looking for others to help you. When you look at the areas of your business that don't excite you quite as much, it is important to hire people that are passionate about those things.

Exercise

You may want to grab a pen and paper or use a digital device to capture your answers as you complete the sentences below (an online version of this can be found at www. thefreedomframework.ca/freegift). Try not to censor yourself or respond in ways you think you should respond. Be honest and be spontaneous. Try and do this exercise quickly. Simply jot down whatever first comes to mind as you complete the sentences.

1. When I was a kid I dreamt of becoming…
2. I can't pass up a book or movie about…
3. If I played hooky from work for a week, I'd spend the time…
4. People don't know this, but I really enjoy…
5. I am the go-to person when my friends or family need help with…
6. If I could star in my own how-to show, it would be about…
7. If I were to make a homemade gift, it would involve…
8. I've only tried it once or twice, but I really enjoy…
9. The closest I have come to experiencing something like a runner's high is when I'm…
10. If I won first place in a talent show, it would be for…

You now have ten separate answers to the ten sentences above. For each group below, pick one answer from your list generated by the sentences above that resonates the most with you and write it down. Try and do this quickly and without too much thought. Trust your intuition or whatever comes to mind first.

- Out of the answers that you provided for questions 1 and 10, which one resonates the most with you?

- Of your answers to questions 2, 3, and 4, which answer most resonates with you?
- Of your answers to questions 5 and 6, which answer stands out the most for you?
- Of your answers to questions 7, 8, and 9, which one jumps out the most at you?

The process above will have narrowed your answers down to four. Of those four answers, above, chose the one that resonates with you the most. This is your passion word or theme.

What Do I Do Now That I Know My Theme?

Once you know your passion word, also known as your theme, you can incorporate that more into the work that you do every day. Once you know the theme for each of the people who work for you, it will be easier to help them get aligned to work that will excite them.

If the theme you identified from above does not immediately make sense to you, identifying your specific passion or theme may require some additional thought. Try doing the exercise again. You can also book a free strategy session to find out how to incorporate your theme into your business by going to www.thefreedomframework.ca/freegift.

Ideally the word you come up with for your theme really resonates with you, and you can see how that theme or passion word can be incorporated into the work you do every day. For example, if your theme is around teaching, you can explore ways to share your knowledge or train others as part of your day-to-day activities. The more time you spend living your theme, the happier you will be.

I had one client who went through this exercise and the word he came up with was "meditation." It made no sense to him and so he assumed that the theme he'd come up with in the exercise was wrong. We dug into it a little deeper. I asked him how he normally started his day. He went early in the morning to a coffee shop and read three newspapers. He really enjoyed quiet time when he could reflect on the things that he learned, refine one to three key points for his team, and then share those learnings. As we talked, it became apparent to him that he was very meditative in his approach as a leader, through his use of deep thought and reflection. Magic! The more he lived his theme of being meditative, the more he could learn and share with his team. I have spoken with many people on his team, and I know they love the time they spend with him in intimate coffee chats, and they gain from the knowledge he shares with them.

Sometimes, when you find out someone's passion word, it may seem difficult to find a linkage between the work they're doing and what they're passionate about. I worked with a leader and his team and there was a woman in his group who was quite disengaged. She seemed very unhappy at work and it got to the point where her negative attitude was rubbing off on others. When they went through this passion exercise as a team, the word that popped out for her was "cookbooks." It turned out that she was really passionate about collecting cookbooks. Her manager asked me how he could help incorporate her passion around cookbooks into the work she did at TELUS, a telecommunications company. Together they determined that she should start a cookbook exchange at work. She brought in cookbooks, which she put on a table behind her desk, and she encouraged others to do the same so that they could share them with each other. Three months later, that woman was bounding into the office with a newfound energy.

It may sometimes seem like a stretch to incorporate someone's personal passions with the work they do. The example of the woman and the cookbooks was somewhat extreme; however, it is still a great example of how her manager helped her with the idea of alignment in the workplace.

Christy, a woman who worked for me, was extremely passionate about technology—in particular about designing and configuring WAN (wide area networks). Christy achieved her networking certification and got 100% on her final test. Working with WAN was what she really wanted to do. The challenge was that Christy was working out in the field at the time and she was not sure how to put her passion for networking to use. I found out about Christy through one of my peers and reached out to her to see if she wanted a role on my team. The small technical team I continued to support was doing *exactly* the kind of work she was passionate about. We brought Christy on board and it was truly amazing to watch her growth and to see her flourish in her new role.

There were fourteen people on that team doing quite complex technical design and provisioning. In less than a year, Christy became one of the two subject matter experts on the team and was supporting people who had been doing that kind of work for over 20 years! That was another great example of how alignment really helped our team and our business by allowing a key resource to live her theme and do work that excited her, while delivering on our goals as a team.

There are many levels of job satisfaction. When you are first starting out, pay and title likely bring you some satisfaction. Over time, however, deeper fulfillment comes from living your theme every day. If problem-solving really excites you and you spend a good portion of your day problem-solving, you will be happier at work. If teaching is your theme and – regardless of what your main role is—you find a way to teach and to share your knowledge with others, you will likely feel better about the work you do.

Finding out what the theme is for each person who works for you, and then helping them spend more time focused on that theme, is key for building committed, passionate teams. This concept holds true regardless of the size of your team.

Summary

Imagine the possibilities if everyone in your business was firing on all cylinders and doing what they loved to do, just like Michael. Imagine working in an environment where everybody was aligned to their theme and to work they were excited about, and how that would impact your team, your customers, your partners, and ultimately your business.

Work satisfaction does not come from having a specific title; it comes from spending time doing the types of things that excite you and give you energy. Imagine what it would feel like to have that type of meaningful alignment, if you don't already have it. Imagine what it would be like to be surrounded with people who were also excited about the work they got to do. One of the greatest measures of success is feeling fulfilled, feeling like you are doing work you are supposed to be doing. The way to achieve this sense of fulfillment—for yourself and for the people who support you—is by aligning with enjoyable work.

Reflection

- As a leader, how do you ensure that your people enjoy their work?
- What would the impact to your business, your team, and your customers be if more people on your team enjoyed more of what they do?
- What does it feel like to do work that you really don't enjoy? How might it impact your business if you had a team that all felt that way?
- Do you know what lights up each one of your team members? How could you shift them toward spending more time working within their themes?

PART 2

THE PEOPLE PLAN

In Part 1 of this book, we discussed that the key to feeling a sense of fulfillment is being in alignment with work you enjoy and getting to "be" in your theme every day. We also reviewed the fact that delivering on some of the other success indicators—such as earning more, having the freedom to focus more of your time on the things that you enjoy, and the flexibility to be where you want to be—can be achieved by hiring the right people to support you and ensuring that they are aligned.

Part 2 is about what to do to support people once you have them in place and they are working in alignment. You have figured out what excites you and where you should spend the majority of your time. You have identified the areas of your business that you are not quite as excited about. And you have hired key people who are passionate about the activities that you are not passionate about. It is not enough to find and hire these people. Your success depends on supporting them to continue to be passionate about working with you and supporting your business goals. Whether leadership is something that comes naturally to you or is the furthest thing from your passion, Part 2 of the Freedom Framework will help you support people to continue to love what they are doing using a People Plan.

What Are the Elements of a Good People Plan?

Designing an amazing workplace starts with alignment. In addition to alignment, there are five other areas of focus required to support an engaged team and create an amazing workplace.

It is important to have a People Plan that addresses all five of these elements:

- the power of people potential
- the value of recognition
- connection through communication
- the desire for continuous improvement
- the impact of giving back

In the next five chapters, we will go into more detail regarding each of these elements.

Regardless of the size of your team, these principles still apply—not only to attract the best talent but to keep them.

Here is a graphic representation of the framework that you can follow to create and support a passionate team:

At TELUS, every year we looked at the high-level categories shown on the model above and decided which specific tactics or initiatives we needed to include for each category. The high-level categories stayed the same, but each year (or sometimes multiple times during a year) we added initiatives to apply them and make them relevant to what was going on with the team, the business issues we were trying to address, what the team needed from us as a leadership team, and what feedback we were receiving.

Why Have a People Plan?

We've talked a bit about four possible success measures in your business. *Financial gain* comes from having yourself or key resources focused on revenue-generating activities instead of administrative tasks. *Fulfillment* comes from ensuring that you and your team are focused on activities that you are each passionate about and that energize you. *Freedom* is a success measure in the sense that you have more time to do the things you want to do, whether they are business-related or not. *Flexibility* is about not having to be in the same location all of the time. All of these results can be better achieved by having a great team of people supporting your business. If you have passionate, engaged people supporting your business who are emotionally connected to your success, that allows you more time to do other things and gives you the flexibility to travel.

Many of my clients see the need to have good people supporting them, but they say that leading people is not their thing. They don't like to have to "babysit" people. They feel that in the time it takes to show someone else how to do something, they might as well just do it themselves. The good news is that whether leading people excites you or not, there is a formula, or framework, that you can follow in order to ensure that your people have the support they need and feel good about being contributors to your business, which, in turn, supports you in your alignment.

The elements in this framework apply whether you have full-time employees, contract resources, volunteers, or a combination. These elements also apply whether you have a team of one person or 10,000. People are people, and the five different categories of the framework apply to all human beings.

CHAPTER 5
The Power of People Potential

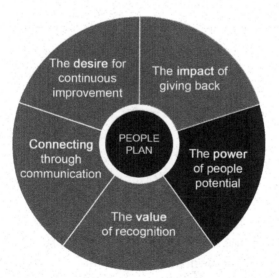

The first of the five components is The Power of People Potential, which includes things like ensuring that your team members have clearly defined career plans and that they are getting the learning opportunities they want and need. There are a number of things that we need to do as leaders in order to ensure our team members' growth and success.

We will review People Potential in detail in this chapter.

What Is the Power of People Potential?

This portion of the People Plan contains aspects that would traditionally be referred to as *human resources* topics. It includes supporting people's growth and development. People need to know that they have opportunities to grow and learn new things and they want to know what career options they have in working with you. If you can help them accomplish their career goals (and, more importantly, their life goals), they will be much more inclined to deliver amazing results for you and your business.

To give you some examples of ways this part of the People Plan can be applied, here are some initiatives we had under the People Potential category, and why they could be beneficial for you to consider for your own company:

Leadership Development

This is a critical subcomponent of a People Plan. If you want to support the growth and evolution of a winning team, the focus needs to be with the leaders, in particular the frontline leaders who support the team on a day-to-day basis. It is one thing to be good at a particular function or to be the best in your business in terms of the job you do, but being a leader takes a completely different skillset. Many organizations promote leaders from within by simply taking the most senior person in a function and then making them the next leader. This may or may not be a good idea. For starters, does that person have any aspirations of becoming a leader? This goes back to alignment and their theme or the types of things they want to focus on. Is leading people their thing?

Leadership development is particularly important for you to address *if leadership is not your thing*. Just because you own a business, that doesn't mean you necessarily need to be the day-to-day leader of it. You may want to be the one who sets the vision and who helps inspire others to help you achieve it, but perhaps you need an operations manager to take care of the team? If someone else is running the show day to day, that's a great way to allow you freedom and flexibility. Hiring an operations manager may be the best way to move you away from the day-to-day activities so you can focus more on revenue-generation or your theme.

When supporting the growth of leaders, there are several skills to address in the overall development plans, such as: coaching, having difficult conversations, financial and business acumen, and performance management, to name a few. Creating a winning culture and nurturing a winning team all start with having the right leaders.

Succession Planning

In order to ensure your success as a team, it is important to do some succession planning. This does not need to be an arduous process. Simply look at the people you have, and in which roles within your organization, and then give some thought as to who would fill those roles should that person move on. For example, if you are a sales-driven organization and your top sales person wants to move on to a different role, what is the plan to fill their position? As part of supporting career growth, encourage everyone to have a plan that starts with where they are now and clarifies where they want to go with their career. Part of making that happen is having a funnel of talent available to help fill the gaps when people move on or up.

We had a mantra in our team at TELUS to remind us that we always wanted to support people to "Move In, Move Up, Move Out."

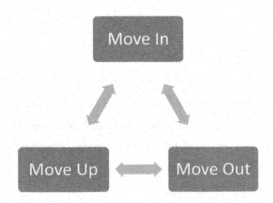

Move In meant that we wanted to attract new talent to our team so that we would always have fresh skills and ideas. Move Up meant that we wanted to be promoting people from within our team to different roles if that was something they wanted as part of their career development. Move Out meant we wanted to be a "net exporter of top talent," as we called it. As we grew and continued to support our team members, we wanted them to freely move on to roles outside of our team in order to expand their skills and help other areas of the company. Succession planning helped us with all of this.

One of the side effects of hiring great people and supporting their growth is that, eventually, they will want to move up and move on. When someone moves up, that may mean moving to a different role within your business, which would be ideal, or it may mean moving to another organization entirely. That is all the more reason to know of other people that you could consider to fill that role, and have a plan for doing so, should the need arise.

Performance Management

People need clear objectives and to know what they are responsible for, and then they need regular feedback about how they are performing against those objectives. It is important for individuals to understand how their objectives tie in with the broader objectives of the company, and how they can contribute to your overall success. This does not need to be a hugely complex process. Having one to three objectives for each team member, and then a plan to meet and discuss them on a regular basis—a minimum of once a month is what I suggest—is key. This is also where effective leadership is required in order to provide feedback on things people are doing well and coaching in the areas where there are opportunities for improvement.

Hiring Practice

I once worked for a leader who said, "You don't drive engagement; you simply hire for it." It took me a while to truly understand what he was talking about, but now I see the merit in what he was saying. If you know the kind of culture you're trying to build, and what kind of team atmosphere you're trying to create, it is important to hire people that fit into that culture. It's one thing to have great technical skills, but if someone is not a fit culturally, you may want to look at other candidates.

We created a strategic hiring plan when trying to elevate our team culture. We had the standard hiring criteria, such as the right post secondary training, job experience, etc., but we also included a number of cultural factors that we wanted any new hire to have. We took a very strategic approach to our hiring and included these factors, amongst others:

- We hired based on situations, not a standard hiring criteria that fit all scenarios.
- We considered the cumulative skills of our team, not only the skills of an individual candidate.

- We looked at not only our short-term needs, but also our long-term needs. This comes back to succession planning and filling the "talent funnel." For example, if we were hiring for a frontline technical role and there were two similar candidates but one of the candidates showed desire and the potential for leadership, we would likely consider them more favorably over the other candidate.

- We considered the candidate's "graduated upskill" potential. Did we see the potential for growing an individual into a resource that we needed in the longer-term?

- We hired based on passion. Is the candidate going to give it their all in terms of effort, and be happy doing so?

We wanted to hire the most talented people, but we also wanted to ensure they were a good fit culturally. I recently heard a business owner saying that she would only hire people she would want to spend eight hours in a car with. I love that! It's another way of saying you want people who will be a good fit for your team and who will contribute to the amazing work environment you are striving to create. For example, if your goal is to have more freedom and flexibility, it is important to hire people that support that goal.

Learning and Development

This was one of most critical areas of employee satisfaction for the teams that I've supported. It was so important that one of the things I did in my People and Culture Champion role was create our own Learning and Development team. It was a small team of three people, but they were wildly successful, as they were able to create learning programs customized for and specific to our team. We were able to assess what our team members needed and then either source existing content or create our own.

Focusing on training for your team is mutually beneficial. Your team members continue to grow and add to their personal toolbox of skills and knowledge, but you as the business owner also benefit from having a highly trained workforce that is continually keeping current with their skills.

At TELUS we had something called a CCDP, or Customized Career Development Plan. It was an amazing tool for helping a manager and team member identify what training the team member needed to take in order to grow as an individual, and also what was needed to support our business goals. The plans were broken down into short-term goals needed for the current role and also longer-term career goals based on where the person wanted to go with their career. We had another mantra in our team, which was that "Personal growth equals business growth." When people are learning, improving their skills, and growing as individuals, it can only benefit your business.

Learning happens in many ways. There is not only learning in a classroom, with an instructor leading the training; there are also other ways of learning. There are many other ways to ensure people's growth, including mentoring, job shadowing, "lunch and learns," webinars, book exchanges, job swapping, and more.

If you have a smaller organization or team, having your own group to create and deliver training may not make sense, but encouraging the people working for you continue to grow and learn does. The more you support a team member's growth, the more loyal they will be to you, and the more ownership they will have in the work they do for you. This can, in turn, help you gain the freedom and flexibility you want.

Summary

The Power of People Potential is the cornerstone of a good People Plan. This is about helping people plan their careers. You help them define their success objectives and you coach them along the way. This is where learning and development opportunities are highlighted so that you are helping people with their growth. The mantra of "Personal growth equals business growth" is a very powerful one. If you help people with their own growth and development, you enhance loyalty and foster an emotional investment that will help your team to stick with you.

Perhaps not all of the initiatives above are relevant for your particular team and situation, but there are benefits to having some measures in place to support not only people's success in their current jobs, but their growth and the business' growth.

Reflection

- What measures do you have in place to ensure that your team members know what is expected of them?
- What needs to be done to clarify what it takes for them to be successful—in the business and in their career?
- What are you doing to ensure that the people you support are getting the training and growth opportunities they need?

CHAPTER 6

The Value of Recognition

Recognition is a key component for supporting a winning team and building a great culture. It can be incredibly powerful if done properly and can be incredibly demotivating if done incorrectly. In this chapter, we will review recognition as the next part of your People Plan.

Acknowledging good work is particularly essential for making employees feel like their work matters. A Globoforce survey found that 69% of employees said they would work harder if they were better appreciated and recognized (Globoforce, 2012).

Several other studies have also emerged around what employees care about at work, including one from Boston Consulting Group (BCG) and The Network, which surveyed over 200,000 people around the world. Unlike previous studies that pointed to flexibility or salary as the top factor for job happiness, this study found that the number one factor for employee happiness on the job was to be appreciated for the work (Rainer et al., 2014).

Is Recognition an Art or a Science?

I once was part of a team where about 60 of us were in an office environment. The general manager at that time was a great guy and he wanted to celebrate the successes of the team by having a pizza luncheon. The challenge was that a number of people on the team did not like pizza or could not eat it due to dietary restrictions. That example has stuck with me for years, because although it was a great attempt at recognition, it fell short for a great many of the team members. The manager's attitude was, "Great job, everyone! I bought you all pizzas to celebrate!" But the team's attitude in response was, "Yes, but we don't really like pizza." The manager had checked off the recognition box, but not everyone was appreciative of his efforts.

Recognition is one of those things that is very personalized. Some people want to be recognized in public, but other people are very uncomfortable with that. One thing we did that was quite successful was create a personalized recognition template for each member of our team. The leadership of the team worked with each team member to discuss and fill out their template, and it became a very powerful tool for keeping track of people's recognition preferences. Simple things were included, like whether they preferred Starbucks or Tim Hortons (a Canada-based coffee and donuts chain), or something else. Those templates went a long way toward ensuring that recognition was meaningful to the individual.

How Do I Best Recognize My People?

We talked about the value of recognition, and that recognition should be personalized. There are some additional best practices when it comes to acknowledging someone for their efforts.

A key element to recognition is timeliness. You want to catch people in the act of doing good and reward it immediately, if you can. Being very specific about the behavior you witnessed and that you are wanting to reward that behavior, ideally creates more of the desired behavior, and this is powerful going forward. Recognition doesn't need to be a formal, grand production. It's often the small gestures that are remembered the most.

As leaders, we can develop a recognition mindset. Like anything else in life, we improve in the things we practice. This may sound extreme, but I used to schedule time in my calendar each day for recognition. I scheduled that time not to be robotic or mechanical about recognizing people, but to ensure that I continually focused on that critical activity. Sometimes I'd send a team member an email about something I thought they would be interested in. I would phone people out of the blue, just to see how they were doing and *not* ask them for anything. I simply wanted to check in with them, and they often told me that blew them away!

Drew Dudley has a great TedX talk called *Everyday Leadership*. I highly encourage you to watch it. It's a stunning example of how the little things we do as leaders can have a massive impact on people.

One of the simplest, yet most powerful, measures we put in place was to have a recognition line item in our budget and make sure leaders knew what that budgeted amount was. We were very specific about the number itself, but not at all prescriptive in how managers used that budget. For example, when we told our leaders that the budget was $15 per person per month, some leaders took their people out for lunch once a month. Some purchased coffee shop or other gift cards each month and handed them out. One innovative leader, through discussions with his team and what they would prefer, purchased gift certificates every month for a fancy restaurant and saved them up. Toward the end of the year, he took his entire team out for a nice dinner, as a way of showing appreciation for their efforts. However leaders chose to utilize it, giving them a number to work with each month was very effective. You can do this, too, by setting aside a budgeted amount every month in your business for recognizing the efforts of your team. The effects of doing so can be very impactful.

Another key to recognition is creating an environment that promotes recognition across your entire team. Many people view recognition as a top-down exercise, but some of the most powerful and meaningful recognition is peer-to-peer recognition. Many companies use electronic platforms to encourage all forms of recognition. At TELUS we had a tool called Bravo, which was world-class quality. Every team member at TELUS could nominate anyone in the company for recognition, based on certain criteria. The cool thing about that platform was that people could accumulate Bravo points and then spend them however they liked, which allowed them to personalize the recognition (to not give someone a Starbucks gift card when they preferred a Tim Horton's one, for example).

As a leader, creating an amazing workplace for your team members is largely about how it feels to go to work every day. Having a culture of recognition can help create an amazing workplace. It just feels good to be acknowledged for your work.

I was speaking recently with one of my clients regarding their People Plan, in particular the recognition component. I asked him about the types of things he had in place from a recognition perspective. His response was, "I pay my people well." I have found that although money is certainly a motivator and a way to recognize people, the effects of it are not as meaningful or long-lasting as other forms of recognition. Paying people well is one form of recognition, but it is table stakes. Getting paid a decent salary in return for hard work is a basic term of employment, not necessarily a world-class way to recognize someone for their efforts. Recognition of the type we're talking about here for your People Plan is more about how you make people *feel* on a day-to-day basis.

A team member helped me on a critical project and his efforts were invaluable to me. I recognized him repeatedly in a number of ways, thinking that I'd done enough. One of the things I always did in my regular meetings with people was to ask them at the end of our session if they had any coaching for me. I found that to be a great way to open up the lines of communication and for me to get feedback about how I could become a better leader. During one of my regular meetings with this man, I asked him if he had any coaching for me. He said he didn't feel appropriately recognized for his efforts on the project he'd helped me with. I was dumbfounded, because I thought I had gone above and beyond with my recognition of him. When I asked him what could have been done differently, he said he wanted to be recognized by our vice president, as the project was important to our whole team. I asked our VP to call him and thank him for his efforts. The fact that the phone call was made after the fact was not ideal, but it was better late than never, and the team member genuinely appreciated the accolades. That was quite an eye-opener for me, as it taught me that recognition can be as simple as making a phone call or thanking someone. It was also a reminder that what we as leaders think is great recognition may not be what the recipient is expecting. Recognition truly is in the eye of the beholder.

It is important to not only recognize the people who work for you but to also recognize your partners and fellow leaders, and—importantly—your clients. Without clients, none of us would have a business or a job, so finding a way to thank clients for their loyalty is crucial.

Have you ever done business with a company that simply thanks you for doing business with them? It feels good that they acknowledge the fact that you could have gone elsewhere but chose to work with them. Another powerful form of recognition of your clients can be in the form of a small gift. Have you ever been to a restaurant where they brought you a little appetizer and did not charge you, simply wanting to thank you for your patronage? Sometimes companies give out little gifts such as pens, USB drives, etc. These things need not be a huge expense item, but the gesture could make a difference. Who doesn't like being recognized with a gift? Recognizing your clients can create long-lasting memories for them of the positive experiences they've had with your company, and can turn your clients into your greatest ambassadors.

Do the Little Things Really Matter?

Here's an example of how everyday leadership that includes a simple and inexpensive recognition of a client can have a big impact.

I was working as a telecom technician, going out to install telephones, ADSL, and TV services for residential clients in their homes. I was working on a very large job in an exclusive West Vancouver neighborhood. A married couple owned the house and they were both home when I was installing their services. I overheard the husband ask his wife, "What would you like to do tomorrow night for your birthday?" I made a mental note of the fact that the woman's birthday was the following day, as I knew I needed to come back for a second day in order to wrap up the installation. There's a small bakery near where I live that bakes the most incredible fresh muffins every morning. The following morning, I stopped by the bakery and grabbed two muffins, one for myself and for the client who was having the birthday. When I knocked on the door and the woman answered, I handed her the muffin and wished her a happy birthday. You would not believe the look of utter surprise on her face. She gave me a big hug, started to cry, and was basically speechless. For the remainder of the day, while I finished the installation, many people called at the house, seemingly to wish her a happy birthday. I overheard her telling the callers, with great enthusiasm, about how the technician knew it was her birthday and so thoughtfully brought her a muffin.

I always think back on that story as another example of how the little forms of recognition can be so powerful. Not only was that woman delighted as a client, but what do you think that simple gesture did in terms of promoting our brand as a company?

Summary
The value of recognition is huge. If done properly, it can lead to retaining your best people and it can lead to a motivated team. Through appropriate recognition, you can develop an emotional connection with the people you support, and they will end up treating your business as if it were their own.

Not acknowledging people in a meaningful fashion is a quick way to demotivate or lose good team members. If someone feels like they have not been appropriately recognized for their efforts, it will not be long before they start looking elsewhere for a job.

Building a mindset whereby recognition becomes part of your leadership DNA and includes your team, your partners, and your clients will help you in all other areas of your business.

Reflection

- How can you create an environment of recognition with your team? How about with your clients?
- What's a system you can set up so that your people have a means of recognizing each other?
- How much are you willing to budget specifically for recognition?
- What are some specific ways you develop a recognition mindset and flex your recognition muscle every day?

CHAPTER 7

Connecting Through Communication

T he next element of the People Plan is Connecting Through Communication. In this chapter, we will review communication and why it is an essential component of supporting a great team that will, in turn, support you and your business.

Why Communicate?

Communication is such an important piece of the puzzle when supporting a team of people (well, pretty much in any aspect of life, really). People need to know what's going on. They need to continually hear from you about the vision, where you are going as a team, and how they fit into that vision.

At TELUS I always said that our communication plan became our engagement plan. By that I simply meant that if we were consistently communicating with our team in a transparent manner and people felt like they knew what was going on, they would be more engaged. In my experience, people just want to feel that they have a voice and that they are part of the conversation.

I remember sitting down with a team of frontline technicians at TELUS and we were talking about some challenges we were going to face as a team. We needed to make some difficult decisions about our structure and other things, in order to address some challenges that had come up. When I sat down with that team, I immediately jumped into the "what"—the details about how I thought we needed to address the challenges. Partway through my spiel, one of the team members stopped me and said, "Cal, you are telling us all the details about what you think we need to do, but you haven't talked about why." That comment stopped me in my tracks. I suddenly realized that the most important element of communicating to a team is the context. The man who had spoken up was 100% correct in that I had not provided the context for the conversation. As a result, what I was saying was not very meaningful for my audience.

When I explained the reasons for having to make the changes we were proposing, that same man said to me, "Why didn't you just say so from the beginning? Give us the why and we will come up with the how." That comment has stuck with me for years. People need context and need to feel like they are part of the conversation, as opposed to being told what to do. From that day forward, I changed my approach and always started with the why when trying to communicate.

It's important for leaders to help translate for their teams, and the best way I have found to do this is by starting with the highest-level context possible and then working down to what it means to the members of the team and then to them as individuals. I refer to this as the "cascading level of contexts."

Back to the TELUS example for a moment. When talking about challenges, I would use this cascading level of context, starting at the global level. I would then move to the Canadian perspective, and then the telecom industry and what the issues of the day meant for it in Canada. I would then shift to the TELUS perspective within the Canadian telecom industry, and then to our broader team within TELUS, and finally to our immediate team and to us as individuals. When you start at the higher levels of context and work down, you can really help people understand things much more deeply and broadly, and that encourages them to be more invested in helping to find solutions and meet challenges.

Communication is similar to recognition, in that it is largely based on the needs of a specific team and individual. What is good for one team or person may not be what another person requires. My experience is that face to face communication is the most effective means of communicating. Whenever we did a survey with our team to see what preferences they had regarding communication, they unanimously said they preferred face to face communication. This can sometimes be a challenge if you have a large team or if your team is geographically dispersed.

Because communicating is such a key component of supporting a team, at TELUS we basically had a plan within a plan. We had our overall People Plan but then also a "communications plan on a page," as we called it, which highlighted the things we wanted to do from a communications perspective. We felt, as a team, that it was so important to us, we had a specific objective for effective communication—"We provide clear and consistent communications to all team members".

I read a quote the other day on the website Communication Theory that I thought summed this up nicely: "The importance of communication can never be over-emphasized. Communication is the 'lifeblood' of all organizations. It is of vital importance to the well-being of a state, a business enterprise, a religion and other social or cultural identities including the family. The success of a business enterprise is directly proportional to the level of communication maintained by it" (Communication Theory).

What Should I Be Doing to Communicate?

Just like with recognition, communication is important for supporting a great team. It also needs to be relevant to your particular business. A number of factors are listed below that we had in our communication plan at TELUS. They may not all be relevant to your business, but they may give you ideas about the types of things you could consider including in your People Plan regarding communication.

Senior Leader Roadshows

This was one of the most effective things we did to stay in touch with our team. We supported team members from coast to coast in Canada, so throughout the year our leadership team planned visits to each location where we had team members so we could have face to face discussions. This was great from the team members' points of view, because they got to spend time with leaders they did not see on a daily basis, but it was also great for us leaders as a way to get feedback from different teams that had different perspectives.

The benefits of doing this type of face to face roadshow are many. The challenge is that—depending on how big your team is and where they are located—it can be costly, and logistically there is a lot of work involved in the planning and organizing of such trips.

When I created the People and Culture Champion role, I wanted to look at other companies I admired for their culture and try and find out more about what they had done to create it. One of the companies that I looked at was Westjet, which is a Canadian airline best known for their great customer service and the ownership mentality of their employees (all of whom are referred to as "owners"). We invited Vito Culmone, who was the Westjet CFO at the time, to come and speak to our team about employee engagement. One of the things he said that was very memorable was, "I have never seen a company that spends so much time on sharing the strategy and vision with its team members as Westjet does." He shared that the senior leadership team at Westjet dedicated three to four weeks per year to travel and visited as many of their team members as possible, in order to share their vision face to face. Those roadshows helped to drive a 91% engagement score, meaning that 91% of the people who worked at Westjet were happy to work there.

Even if you have a small team, setting up time to regularly share your insights and vision with your team can go a long way.

Weekly Conference Call

I found this to be *hugely* valuable for supporting my team. In particular, when we were all working in different locations, having that regular, weekly touch point was very important for keeping us connected as a team. These conference calls can be done as phone calls or as video calls.

We had our call every Monday afternoon at the same time for about five years straight. Because the calls were held at the same time every week, everyone knew ahead of time when the calls would be, and so they were always there. We would review our success measures as a team in order to ensure that we were on track, but the calls also gave us a chance to joke with each other a bit and an opportunity to simply check in. We used an audio conference bridge for the calls, but we also used Webex so we could share our respective screens. I would often do things like ask people to share their pictures from the weekend (no X-rated ones, though!) or to share something personal about themselves.

For a team that's not physically with each other every day, such calls can be very valuable in keeping everyone connected.

Mid-Year and Year-End Videos

Creating and sharing these videos were great tools for celebrating our successes as a team. The videos were done in a very emotional, impactful manner and were very touching. We included updates on our key operational metrics, which was necessary for showing our progress from a business perspective, but we also included other elements, such as pictures of our team members engaged in community giving events, pictures of people's families (one of our managers, for example, had twin baby girls and we included a picture of him with his newborn twins), and pictures of our team members working in cool places such as on the tops of mountains. Everybody on the team looked forward to the release of those videos because they were cool. But they were also a key component of our communications plan. They kept people in the loop and highlighted the great things we accomplished together as a team.

One of the challenges of creating videos such as these is simply collecting the content. We had someone on our team who could do all of the creation and editing of the video (Michael, whom I mentioned earlier in the book), but it was sometimes a challenge to gather all the input required. There is also a cost involved and, obviously, the time needed to create the video. Nevertheless, we considered it worthwhile, because it was such an impactful way to make an emotional connection with our team.

Daily or Weekly Team Huddles

Team huddles are a very informal yet very effective way to communicate with your team. We would have a daily huddle, first thing in the morning, and give people an opportunity to ask questions or share concerns. We would also review the goals for the day for us as a team, to ensure that everyone was on the same page. It's a fantastic way to ensure that everyone is focused on the right activities.

Anonymous Surveys

We offered team members the chance to take part in anonymous surveys. We wanted to get feedback from the team and ensure that *everyone* had an opportunity to voice their opinions. We also wanted the feedback to be completely honest and candid. Among the various other ways we collected feedback, we launched a quarterly survey that was 100% anonymous. The feedback we got as a result of those surveys was incredible. Many times I'd thought I had my finger on the pulse of the team, but then was surprised by the comments we received from those surveys. I learned about things that I hadn't thought of, different and new perspectives on issues, and much more.

If you do not currently have a method for your team to give you completely honest feedback without there being any repercussions, I highly recommend implementing one. We were able to take those quarterly survey results and determine whether the initiatives we had launched were delivering value to our team, and to see if we needed to scrap or alter some things.

———————

In addition to the suggestions above, here a few other things that we tried in terms of fostering good communication:

- Podcasts
- Year-end messages from senior leaders
- Launching a Sharepoint site to share information among the team

- Monthly calls with all of our managers, to review results, and discuss strategy and culture
- Monthly calls focused exclusively on people and culture, during which we would discuss how we supported our team and where things stood from a culture point of view. Those calls were great, because we kept them separate from our regular operational meetings and that ensured that we discussed nothing but our team.
- Generating Key Messages slides every month that our managers could share with their teams.
- Hosting Beer and Dinner Nights. These were also very successful (perhaps for obvious reasons), as our team members got to meet with our leadership team in an informal setting, which helped them feel more comfortable sometimes to ask any questions they may have.
- Hosting informal town hall type meetings. When any of our leaders traveled to a different city or location for a meeting, we set aside informal time for them to have discussions with the teams.
- Celebrating customer service week and communicating our successes to the team.
- Year end messages from our vice president.

Summary

Communication is so important when supporting a team. It is such a huge contributor to how people feel about working in a particular company, and to whether or not they feel like they are valued and a part of the team. In my experience, communications are much stronger when there's a plan in place to support them, and when there are dedicated time and resources to ensure an appropriate focus.

Reflection

- How do you regularly communicate with your team?
- What's a way you could get candid feedback on what you are doing well and on where you could perhaps improve?

CHAPTER 8

The Desire for Continuous Improvement

When building a passionate team, striving to continuously grow and improve is a key factor. In this chapter, we will discuss continuous improvement as the next step in creating a great People Plan.

Why Strive to Continuously Improve?

William S. Burroughs said, "When you stop growing, you start dying." This definitely applies in business, too. If we are not continually trying to grow and improve, we risk becoming complacent, which is never a good thing.

During my work as the People and Culture Champion at TELUS, my philosophy of team engagement was that we started from scratch at the beginning of every year. I used to suggest to our leaders that every year, on January 1st, our engagement score reset to zero percent. My point was that we couldn't rest on our laurels, even if we had done great things to support the team in the year before.

You may have heard of the Japanese term *kaizen*. Kaizen is a practice of continuous improvement. Some of the aspects of this practice are as follows:

- Having good processes can create good results. (How we continually improve on our processes will help us continually improve our results.)
- Go see the processes for yourself. (If you actually get to do the job as a leader, you can help determine where to make improvements.)

- Speak with data, manage by facts. (This speaks to having great measurements around your company's processes so the data will inform you about where you can potentially make improvements.)
- Work as a team. (Together, everyone can be part of the solution for making things better.)
- Continuous improvement is everybody's business. (We can all contribute to making things better every day.)

One of the most notable features of having a continuous improvement practice like Kaizen or otherwise is that small improvements over time can result in big changes. I love this! I sometimes got overwhelmed by all the initiatives and things I wanted to do to support our team, but simply going back to the idea that big results can come from many small changes helped to keep me grounded. I constantly asked myself, *What small thing can I do today, right now, that will help make tomorrow better?*

One of my business clients has something they refer to as the "Stellar Experience Culture." They use the adjective "stellar" as their desired benchmark to gauge everything they do. They believe that one of the key areas for success in their business is having a passion for creating outstanding, positive, and memorable experiences for not only their clients but also their team members. After every interaction with his team, my client asks himself if that interaction was stellar and, if not, what he could do differently to be better the next time.

This is a fantastic example of a way to foster a continuous improvement mindset and to foster a stellar culture within your organization.

How Do I Continually Improve My Business?

Many people would agree that trying to continuously improve as an individual and as an organization is a valuable thing to do. The challenge sometimes is knowing *what* to do. I am often asked the question, "Improvement sounds great, but *how* do we know what to focus on?" The following is an approach for answering this question. It's an approach we used when I worked at TELUS.

The leadership team used to sit in a boardroom with a whiteboard and try to come up with things we thought our team would like to see. It dawned on me at one point that the best way to find out what our team would like to see for improvements would be to simply ask them! That sounds so simple, but we sometimes overlooked the power of asking our team directly what would make them feel better about working there.

Based on our asking and the team's answers, we implemented many ways to collect feedback from our team, including a formal, annual Pulsecheck survey, the quarterly ongoing anonymous surveys I spoke of in the previous chapter, as well as many other formal and informal means. We would then take the top three opportunities as identified by our team and come up with plans to take action on those items. The cool thing about the process was that we had engagement primes from each of the teams who would help to create and execute the plan, so the process was inclusive and we had buy in from the team members themselves. Those primes were individuals who were passionate about supporting other people and making our organization a better place to work. Through this approach, we had representation from a number of different areas and could get a much broader perspective as a result, which helped us with our leadership.

Here's an example of this process. We reviewed our survey results from 2014 and the top three areas of opportunity that the team wanted to work on were:

1. Learning and Development
2. Career Opportunities
3. Work Processes

We pulled together the primes from each area, looked at those three opportunities, and created initiatives around each of them that the team felt would make a difference.

To address learning and development, we created our own learning team that would drive the development opportunities the team wanted to see. We also created a consolidated view of all of our learning demand—for example, the courses everyone wanted to take in order to support our business goals—and then ensured that everyone got at least some of the training they wanted in that year.

One of the most important factors in job satisfaction, over and above salary, is learning and growth. If people are learning and growing, feeling like they're staying current and relevant, they will be much more loyal and productive to your company.

To address work processes, we created an online tool that allowed people to identify any opportunities they saw to make an improvement in the way we served our clients. People could submit their ideas online, and then we had incentives for coming up with the best ideas to pursue. We also had a way of tracking the submissions to ensure that every idea was responded to. We felt it was critical that, if our team was bringing forth ideas, they need to be kept updated about their submission, whether their suggestion was implemented or not. We felt it was as important to acknowledge that they had submitted something, and to communicate with them about the status of their submissions, as it was to actually explore implementing what they had suggested. We developed a way to produce reporting that showed how many submissions had been made, what the improvements were as a result of those submissions, and what the overall impact had been.

Having processes such as those went a long way toward enhancing our continuous improvement mindset. Our team members felt some ownership in our business and that we all had an equal opportunity to make the company and our team a better place to work.

Regarding the issue of team members not knowing what opportunities were available to them, one of the biggest pieces of feedback was that our team members had a general sense that there were opportunities for them, but they did not know specifically which opportunities they could pursue. We created something we called the Career Path Matrix tool, which showed which jobs were out there, what type of skills were needed to do those jobs, and people who could be contacted to find out more about the jobs. That tool was impactful because it gave people a clear sense of the jobs that were available and also showed them what it would take to get one of those jobs. Perhaps you have a very small team and so you don't have a tool such as the one above. You can still let people know what opportunities they can look forward to when they come and work with you. It is hugely helpful to let people know what is available and to support what they are working toward in their career. This leads to long-term retention and loyalty, as people see that they can grow with you and your company, not only by focusing on the role they have today, but also by having a clear understanding of what the future may hold for them.

Summary

The approach of having a plan about continuous improvement may seem like overkill, especially if you have a very small team, but asking yourself how to improve on the things you do is always valuable. Your approach to always trying to get better could be as simple as asking your team what is important to them, asking them how they would like to see these things improve over time, and then having a means of working on those things and a way of showing and sharing progress.

By really taking ownership and trying to make continuous improvements, we saw a 13% improvement in the survey results around learning and development, a 10% improvement in career opportunities, and a 12% improvement in work processes, from 2014 to 2015. We also saw our overall team engagement score improve by 7%. Those results speak to the value of having continuous improvement as part of your People Plan, and the value of creating an exceptional work environment.

Reflection

- What's a method that appeals to you for fostering continuous growth and improve in your business?
- How can you capture the improvement items that are important to your team and business? How can you act upon them? How can you share the results over time?

CHAPTER 9

The Impact of Giving Back

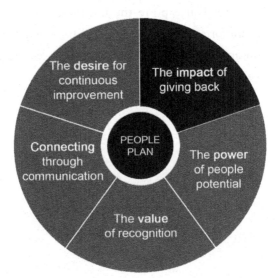

I n this chapter, we review the importance of community giving as part of a People Plan, and how it helps create an exceptional team environment.

Why is Giving Back Important?

Who hasn't heard the saying "It's better to give than to receive"? Giving of yourself to others is one of the most human of things we can do. In business today, giving in the communities in which we work and serve is also critical to success. Clients want to know that you are a business with heart and that you care about more than the bottom line—particularly if your clients are in the 18 to 34 age range, because that age group now makes up the largest demographic on the planet, surpassing even baby boomers.

A study conducted by Cone Communications revealed that nine in ten Millennials would switch to a brand associated with a good cause. Additionally, 70% would pay more for a product or take a pay cut to work for a responsible company (66%). Millennials are one of the most sought after target audiences today, and their collective purchasing power measures in the hundreds of billions! They are noted for approaching business and capitalism with a conscience, so to win them over it's important to do so through the action of giving. (Cone Communications Inc., 2015)

Community giving is important for attracting clients and for bringing a human heart into business, but it is also crucial for attracting the best talent. In today's job market, many people seek out companies to work for that are aligned with their own giving perspectives. Allowing your employees to be involved in some sort of charity work used to be a nice thing to do. Now it is absolutely imperative.

I have a business client that epitomizes the concept of community giving, for both their clients and their employees. They consider themselves a company with heart. In fact, giving is so important to them that their entire business has been built around it. They have something they call the Mission of Care. If you book an appointment to see one of their strategists, the company will donate $100 to a charity of your choice, whether you do business with them or not. This program is great for their business as well as for their customers ("friends" are what this company calls their customers). It feels different as a client when you interact with a company that puts giving first. When booking an appointment with this company, the fact that the conversation starts with discussing a cause that you are passionate about, as opposed to jumping into a discussion about purchasing products you may or may not need, sets that company apart from their peers.

In defining their beliefs around giving, here is what they came up with: "We have always thought of ourselves as a financial services company with a lot of heart. We know that in order to excel in business, we need to give back to the communities in which we live and work. We believe everyone wants to give back and experience the joy of giving. We believe that it is our responsibility to make the world a better place and we want to inspire our clients to make the world a better place along with us."

The Mission of Care concept is a great way to attract new clients and to help your team members engage those clients. You can book a free session with me to learn more about how this concept can help your business. To do so, go to www.thefreedomframework.ca/freegift.

That particular company also had a number of other initiatives around community giving. All of their initiatives combined ensured that giving was part of their company's DNA. Those giving activities, in particular the Mission of Care, reflected in their bottom line. They had extremely good metrics around how the number of Mission of Care conversations their strategists had with prospective clients equated to revenue. This is a great reminder that giving is not only the right thing to do, it's also definitely good for business.

How Do I Win the Hearts and Minds of My Team?

One of the keys to building a great culture within your company is having an emotional connection with the people who work for you. Community giving is one of the best ways of building this connection. At TELUS we had a saying: "We Give Where We Live." Like many companies, TELUS gives back to the communities they serve. An impressive example of this was the TELUS Day of Giving (sometimes it was multiple days), in which the entire TELUS team had the opportunity to volunteer their time for causes they believed in. I was always amazed at the connections I made with my team when we volunteered on those days.

When you can get your team out of the workplace (and invite their friends and family along) to go try and make the world a better place, the relationships and bonds built together are invaluable.

Another key element to getting this emotional buy-in about giving in the workplace is to not be too prescriptive about giving with your team. You may have company-wide charitable activities that everyone is expected to participate in, but giving people some autonomy and a chance to choose how they support a charity, or to support a cause that they are really passionate about, is another way to show support for that team member and to build a connection.

One of the workshops I run with my clients is around Meaningful Alignment and helping people connect things that are important to them personally with the work they do. There are some simple but extremely powerful exercises we do in this workshop that help leaders and their teams make this connection. One is the Perfect Day exercise (as seen in an earlier chapter), in which people think about their perfect day (or a day that was very memorable for them). The vast majority of time, the memories people describe are from days that involved giving to or helping others. I am reminded of a time when my wife and I took a trip to the Caribbean island of Antigua. We had an amazing time and did all kinds of cool things, scuba diving, touring some historical sites, going to a great reggae BBQ, and sailing a 60-foot racing yacht, launching it off the waves in the turquoise blue water. But we also arranged to spend a day in a school with some special-needs children. My wife and I volunteered for the day and spent time giving of ourselves with those amazing children. The experience we had was so moving that it kind of made me forget about all the other activities we had done on our trip, because the volunteering felt the most meaningful. When I think back on that trip, I don't usually think about those other activities (well, I do envision being out on that racing yacht!), but I do think about the day we spent volunteering.

How Does Giving of My Time Help?

"Giving" can take on many forms. We often think of the obvious volunteering examples such as the ones listed above, but one of the most powerful forms of giving, for a leader, is simply giving unconditionally of your time. When I called people who worked for me out of the blue, just to check in and ask them how they were doing, that felt energetically different from calling them when I needed them to do something. Taking team members for coffee or lunch and *not* talking about work is another way to give of your time. I found that what people craved from me the most was my time and my willingness to be present with them. Keep this in mind as a great way you can give as a leader.

Summary

There is a real benefit to you as a business owner to incorporate giving into your team culture. If you think about most of the well-known and respected brands on the planet, they each have a huge element of corporate giving. Companies like Google, Virgin, Apple, Expedia, and Microsoft donate countless hours and dollars to causes they care about. They know it's the right thing to do, but they also know that it's good for business.

Community giving as part of your culture is about the feeling it invokes—how it feels as an employee to work for a company that cares, and how it feels as a client to know that the company you deal with has heart. As a business owner, when you supporting giving it positively impacts profit, and you can take pride in the fact that you have made a difference. That all feels pretty good, doesn't it?

Reflection

- How can you incorporate more giving into the culture at your company?
- How might you, your employees, and your clients feel if your company and the team did more giving?

CHAPTER 10

The Challenge of Creating a Winning Team

D elivering on all success measures in your business is achievable. It is possible to be successful financially but also to be fulfilled by the work you do. It is also possible to have more time to do the things you love to do and be able to do them from wherever you like. The way to do this is by unlocking the passion and potential of the people who work for you, and by focusing on how it "feels" to your clients or customers to do business with you.

Having a plan to, first, support alignment for yourself and your people, and then having a People Plan that includes all the other elements of supporting a highly motivated and inspired team is not only possible, it's a real Freedom

Framework. Of course, this freedom does not come without challenges. In my experience, some of the challenges of creating a dream culture for your business that supports your freedom are as follows.

<u>Leadership</u>

Perhaps you have a small company and you are the only leader. If this is the case, first consider how aligned are you and look at the tools you already have in place to ensure that you are consistently checking in with your team, determining if they are doing work that lights them up, and taking care of the other elements of supporting a team. Then see what you can add. Taking small steps can reassure you that you're moving in the appropriate direction. The steps will add up and combine to give you a greater result. Without a framework to keep yourself on track as a leader regarding these factors—recognition, performance potential (seeing how people are doing against their objectives and coaching them to be their best), getting team members the learning and development that they need, etc.—it can be challenging to ensure that you always have an appropriate level of focus on your team.

If you have a larger organization where there are more leaders than only yourself, continued focus can be a real challenge. Some leaders naturally gravitate toward the care of their teams, but for others that care does not come as naturally. Even if you do have a natural tendency toward caring for your teams, how do you ensure that you are continually focusing on your people and giving them the support that they require? With our often hectic schedules as leaders, and with dealing with all other aspects of our businesses—such as sales, marketing, operations, and finance—what structures can we put in place to make sure our team members are happy and our business thrives, with or without our constant presence? This is a big question. The Freedom Framework outlined in this book gives you a plan to follow to create that structure.

Planning

An engaged team does not happen by accident. (I know I sound like a broken record). Many business owners have marketing plans, sales plans, contingency plans, business plans, and all kinds of other plans. I often ask business owners (not to be a jerk, but just out of curiosity), "What is your People and Culture plan?" Not every business has one. Due to the intangible nature of dealing with people ("soft skills"), it can be challenging to create a plan. In my experience, it is extremely challenging to build a winning culture and have an engaged team without it. But the benefits of having a functioning Freedom Framework are worth the cost of putting one into place in your business.

Losing Some People Along the Way

One of the perhaps unexpected outcomes of creating a kickass culture and developing a winning team is churn. I did an "alignment workshop" with a client in Australia, in early 2016. Garry was the owner of a small IT company in Melbourne. He was a heartfelt leader who believed in supporting the growth of his people unconditionally. He wanted to have a day that was all about *them* and focused on their passions, and then align their passions and the things that were important to them personally with the work that they did at his company. It was obvious to me that he was clearly very excited about the workshop.

As we were planning for the workshop, I mentioned to Garry in a phone call that I wanted to give him a warning of a possible outcome. "Garry, I need to warn you that one of the outcomes of this alignment work could be that you lose some people." There was a silent pause on the phone and then came Garry's response of, "Yes, but is that not a good thing?" I was so pleased to hear him say that! It may not be easy to lose good people from your organization; however, if there are people on your team who are not doing the work they should be doing, that can have a negative effect on team culture. Not everyone will be a fit for what you are trying to create, so you may have to part ways with some people as part of this process of alignment. The good news is that you can incorporate alignment into your hiring practices to ensure that people are a good fit from the beginning, so hopefully you do not have to let people go later.

It Takes Effort

We used the measure of engagement as a barometer of how people were feeling at work. The engagement score we used was comprised of collated answers to six questions in three different categories: stay, say, and thrive. Stay was a retention measure of how likely it was that people would stay with the company. Say was about what team members said about the company to their friends and family. Thrive basically measured the degree to which people felt like they were inspired to do their best. The results of the answers to the six questions combined gave an "engagement score" or, in simple terms, an indication of how happy people were at work.

I mentioned this earlier in the book, but I'll say it again here as a reminder: Consider resetting your company's engagement score to zero at the beginning of every year. Keeping a team engaged takes effort, and that reset to zero gives you a fresh start. Our businesses and our teams are constantly changing; therefore, our approach to supporting a dynamic team needs to continue to change also. What was important to a particular team member last year may not be the same this year. It pays to always be thinking about how we can raise the bar and support people to love what they do. The outcome we want is for them to be champions for your company.

It Can Be Hard To Measure

Peter Drucker and many others have said, "What gets measured gets done." Supporting a team and creating a world class culture is no exception. Having a framework in place and a means of measuring your people initiatives is key. The challenge that I have encountered with this is that identifying metrics that relate to how people *feel* can be challenging. You may have other key performance indicators for your business, such as how many sales calls are made each month, how many widgets you manufacture, etc. These are all very clear-cut measurements. When it comes to measuring a culture, though, what does that look like?

You can use a Cultural Scorecard, which is an index for measuring a number of initiatives that you think should lead to an engaged team. When I work with my clients on this, we include things like ensuring that team members have the appropriate learning and development, have clearly defined career paths, and are being recognized for their efforts (all the elements from the People Plan, as described in the previous chapters). This scorecard is a great indicator of engagement, but there are two other means of measuring culture that can be even more effective.

One is to ask people how they feel. Doing a survey and carefully considering what questions to ask your team about the overall culture and how they feel working at your organization can be very powerful as the answers start coming in. You can have all of the facts, data, and numbers that you want, but when you really check in with your team and get feedback about how they feel, that is often the best indicator of how engaged and happy they are at work, and that is a great indicator of the health of your culture.

The second means of measuring comes from using your own intuition as a leader. As leaders, we often know when someone is showing up at work and giving it their all versus when they are not quite there. We can further develop this emotional quotient, or EQ, in order to really tune in to how people feel about the company. In your ongoing one-on-one conversations with team members, if you know the right questions to ask—meaning questions that get you useful answers—you can stay apprised of the status of the culture and the level of engagement. This is an ongoing exercise, but a hugely valuable one.

Creating a winning team is not easy and it doesn't happen overnight. It takes focus and forethought. It takes a commitment from leaders to build something bigger than the bottom line. I have seen countless examples of companies that achieve and surpass all of their business objectives by putting alignment into effect and making supporting their teams a top priority. You can do this, too!

Reflection

- In what ways do you think creating and supporting a passionate team would help you with your business?
- How much does your current team and business environment allow you the fulfillment, flexibility, and freedom you desire?

CHAPTER 11
Your Freedom Framework

What can being aligned and having a great team do for your business? It can do everything! Having a great culture—meaning you have a great team that loves what they do—can help you overcome any business challenge and meet any business objective. It can also allow you to have the business you've always dreamed of: having a business that's financially strong; being fulfilled in the work you do; having a team that supports your business so that you can focus on more valuable activities; and having some freedom to travel and work remotely when you like. A passionate team will also go the extra mile to serve your customers. Your customers, in turn, will feel good about their experience, making it more likely that they will tell their friends and family about the experience they had when dealing with your team.

Being aligned with work you're passionate about and having a great team to support other areas of your business can have a huge impact. Below are some of the success measures that will be positively impacted in your business through the process of putting your Freedom Framework into place.

Productivity

This is going to increase if people are aligned with work they love. When people are doing what they were meant to do, they will be willing to go the extra mile for you. When a person is doing what they love and work doesn't feel like work because they are so passionate about what they're doing, it stands to reason that they will do more of it.

Attracting Investors

Investors are attracted to companies that have a great culture and great people. You may be the best basket manufacturer on the planet, but if you don't have that "X factor" or give people who deal with your company a great feeling, investors will look elsewhere. If you've ever watched the TV show *Shark Tank*, have you noticed how many times the Sharks say they want to invest because they believe in the person and what they are doing? That is, in part, because of the company's culture and it's a result of that person's alignment. When you are aligned, people will want to do business with you, because they will feel that you are passionate about what you do.

Attracting Talent

The brightest and best talent want to be part of something cool and not just get a paycheck. The millennial generation, in particular, seeks out companies that have a cool culture and that address all of the elements covered in this book (including career growth opportunities, giving, alignment, communication, recognition, and continuous improvement). They seek out companies that are known for their great culture because they want to feel good every day about the work they do.

I remember the last person I hired when I was at TELUS. I called her in for an interview, but I felt like she interviewed me! She wanted to know what I stood for and what kind of culture had been created in the team she would be joining. She wanted to know that she would be given work that was meaningful to her and that she would get a sense of fulfillment from her job. There is a big shift toward putting people and their growth first and everything else afterward. We, as leaders, need to be aware of this shift and stay on top of it.

Bottom Line

The bottom line is that your profits will increase when you create a culture that fosters a highly motivated, passionate team that is aligned around what is important to them personally and the work they do for your company. A study by Gallup showed that workers who were in the top percentile of engagement (meaning they enjoyed what they did and where they worked) produced 22% more profitability (Sorenson, 2013). There is a tangible benefit to your balance sheet by putting culture first.

———————

I envision a world where everybody gets to do the work they were meant to do, and where visionary leaders grow their businesses by putting people first. I believe in the powerful mantra that "Personal growth equals business growth." By helping people get aligned with work they're excited about, and supporting their growth process, you can create an amazing culture in your workplace.

Creating a People Plan for your company will help you thrive in all other areas of your business and your life.

Thank you for taking the time to read this book, and for helping make the possibility of alignment for more business leaders and teams a reality.

References

Rainer Strack, Carsten von der Linden, Mike Booker, and Andrea Strohmayr, "Decoding Global Talent," BCGPerspectives.com, October 6, 2014. www.bcgperspectives.com/content/articles/human_ resources_leadership_decoding_global_talent/? chapter=5.

Communication Theory, "Importance of Communication to Organisations or Importance of Business Communication," CommunicationTheory.org. http://communicationtheory.org/importance-of-communication-to-organisations-or-importance-of-business-communication.

Cone Communications Inc., "New Cone Communications Research Confirms Millennials As America's Most Ardent CSR Supporters, But Marked Differences Revealed Among This Diverse Generation," ConeComm.com, Sep 23, 2015.

www.conecomm.com/news-blog/new-cone-communications-research-confirms-millennials-as-americas-most-ardent-csr-supporters.

Fermin, Jeff, "10 Shocking Stats About Disengaged Employees," Officevibe.com, January 2014.

www.officevibe.com/blog/disengaged-employees-infographic.

Globoforce Mood Tracker Survey was conducted by Globoforce from March 16-19, 2012.

www.globoforce.com/resources/research-reports/mood-tracker-spring-2012-the-growing-influence-of-employee-recognition.

Shriar, Jacob, "14 Disturbing Employee Engagement Statistics," Officevibe.com, July 25, 2016.

www.officevibe.com/blog/disturbing-employee-engagement-infographic.

Sorenson, Susan, Gallup Business Journal, "How Employee Engagement Drives Growth," Gallup.com, June 20, 2013.

www.gallup.com/businessjournal/163130/employee-engagement-drives-growth.aspx.

Acknowledgments

First, I want to thank some of the mentors I've had throughout my career. Thanks to Dave McMahon for being an inspiring leader and showing me that we really can do things our own way while also having the integrity to say what needs to be said and to care about people. His leadership regarding mentoring people will always be with me.

Thanks to Marshall Berkin for believing in me and allowing me to "do my thesis." His encouragement means a great deal. Having his help to move on to supporting people's growth and focusing on people and culture is one of the best examples of "meaningful alignment" I can think of.

Thanks to Michael Thomas for always being there and for helping to solidify the content around alignment and people/culture. He is always there for me, and I look forward to having more of our passionate discussions around how to make the world a better place by helping people do work that they love.

I send out a huge debt of gratitude to Sean Richardson for helping me make sense of my ideas around alignment and what it takes to support a team of people. Thanks to him also for showing me what was possible, and for believing in me, even when I had some doubts myself.

Thanks to Joe Roberts for his counsel and for helping me to believe that I can accomplish anything I set my mind to. I also appreciate our "roadside chats" and look forward to many more of them (minus watching him spit his crown into the palm of his hand!).

Thanks to Garry Busowsky for offering me my first post-corporate gig and for inviting me to Melbourne, Australia, so I could truly call myself an international consultant! The unconditional support he showed for the growth of his team truly inspires me.

Thanks to Scott Low for showing me that there really are heartfelt leaders out there who understand that it's possible to grow a business and still care deeply about people. I also thank him for allowing me to work with his organization and to create something truly special.

My sincere gratitude goes to Philip McKernan for helping me reconnect with myself, and for helping me find the courage to go out and do what I was truly meant to do. His work really does matter, and I am deeply appreciative of how he has helped me. Thanks to him also for writing the foreword to this book. I could not think of a person I would more like to have write it than him.

To the Morgan James Publishing team: Special thanks to David Hancock, CEO & Founder for believing in me and my message. To my Author Relations Manager, Margo Toulouse, thanks for making the process seamless and easy. Many more thanks to everyone else, but especially Jim Howard, Bethany Marshall, and Nickcole Watkins.

Lastly, thanks to my wife, Jane, for her unconditional support. I know that my many schemes have often created discomfort for her, but she has always recovered with grace, and she always asked how she can help. I am sure it has not been easy dealing with my many and often multi-directional pursuits, but I hope, at the end of the day, that at least she will say that life has never been dull. I thank her, again, for having my back.

About the Author

Cal Misener is a consultant, coach, facilitator, and international speaker who is passionate about helping individuals and organizations achieve alignment between what is important to them personally and the work they do, as well as the impact they want to make.

Cal has over 20 years of experience in business environments. His core strengths including leadership, communication, and developing deep connections with people.

Cal has gone through his own personal transformation of doing work that he was not very excited about, and now he focuses exclusively on his passion for helping others achieve meaningful alignment in their lives. He has supported the transformation of hundreds of people to become more aligned in their lives. In doing so, he created the Freedom Framework, which can also help you and your organization, regardless of its size.

Cal is a man of many pursuits, including being outdoors, traveling, fishing, cooking, and, especially, music. He currently lives with his wife on an island off of Canada's west coast.

Website: www.thefreedomframework.ca
Email: HOMESHOP@telus.net
Linkedin: www.linkedin.com/in/calmisener

Thank You

Thank you very much for taking the time to read this book. As you probably know by now, I'm extremely passionate about helping people with alignment and ensuring that they are passionate about the work that they do. For years, I did work that did not serve me very well and I can assure you that it feels much better when you are aligned!

This book is just the beginning of a journey of discovering what truly lights you up and then creating the business of your dreams around that passion.

To further encourage you, I've put together resources that will be valuable as you continue on your journey. Included in this resource material is a free copy of the Passion Exercise, as shown in Chapter 4. There's also a free assessment you can do to determine where you are in terms of the various success measures in your business.

To access these resources, go to
www.thefreedomframework.ca/freegift.

Thanks again,
Cal

Morgan James
Speakers Group

www.TheMorganJamesSpeakersGroup.com

We connect Morgan James published authors with live and online events and audiences who will benefit from their expertise.